WHAT GOD IS SAYING

Object Lessons from the Prophets for Kids

Anne Marie Gosnell

What God is Saying: Object Lessons from the Prophets for Kids

© 2023 Anne Marie Gosnell. All rights reserved. Permission is given to use said document in a home, school, church, or co-op setting. This document may not be transmitted in any other form or by any other means—electronic, mechanical, photocopying, recording, or otherwise—without prior written permission of Anne Marie Gosnell. Coloring pages may be copied for classroom lessons.

ISBN: 978-1-7351329-3-8 (print)

Scripture quotations taken from the New American Standard Bible® (NASB), Copyright © 1960, 1962, 1963, 1968, 1971, 1972, 1973, 1975, 1977, 1995 by The Lockman Foundation. Used by permission. www.Lockman.org

The Holy Bible, English Standard Version (ESV) is adapted from the Revised Standard Version of the Bible, copyright Division of Christian Education of the National Council of the Churches of Christ in the U.S.A. All rights reserved.

ICB — Scripture taken from the International Children's Bible®. Copyright © 1986, 1988, 1999 by Thomas Nelson. Used by permission. All rights reserved.

Publishing and Design Services: MartinPublishingServices.com

"In a time when so few kids know how to read and understand the Bible, *What God is Saying* provides teachers with exactly what they need to help kids grow spiritually. It's engaging, deeply Bible-based, and will create rich conversations around Bible passages kids may never have encountered before. A great resource for any Sunday school or classroom teacher!"

—**Christie Thomas**, award-winning author of
Fruit Full: 100 Family Experiences for Growing in the Fruit of the Spirit

"*What God is Saying* provides hands-on ways for kids to learn about and understand the prophets—an often difficult portion of the Bible even for adults. I appreciate how the book takes big truths and simplifies them for kids without losing the significance of the scriptural text, and the background and geography sections for each lesson give context to the lesson and Bible teaching so kids have a framework for what they're learning. These easy-to-lead object lessons create opportunities for deeper discussions for kids about how God spoke in the past and how He can speak today. Highly recommend!"

—**Brittany Nelson**, Founder & Creator, Deeper KidMin

"Anne Marie does it again with this amazing resource for bible teachers. With engaging bible lessons guaranteed to ignite the imagination of children, Anne Marie helps bible teachers present the truth of God in a way that sticks. From the Old Testament to the New, she provides creative object lessons that are accessible and easy to use for any and all Bible teachers irrespective of their level or experience. Definitely a must have for every leader who teaches the Bible to children."

—**Esther Moreno**, Founder Child's Heart LLC

"*What God is Saying: Object Lessons from the Prophets for Kids* by Anne Marie Gosnell is packed full of powerful lessons that bring a message of hope to children. The only thing I love more than telling kids about God's Word is showing it to them too, and the object lessons in this book do exactly that. Whether you're in children's ministry or you're a parent or guardian looking to make a Kingdom-sized impact in a kid's life, this book is a great resource!"

—**David Rausch**, Founder and President
of Go Tell It LLC and Creator of GO! Curriculum

DEDICATION

To Eric,

I don't have the right words to say thank you.
You are my best friend.

I love you.

CONTENTS

Introduction 3

How This Book Works 4

A Few Last Tips 6

What is a Prophet? 7

The Calling of Samuel 14

Nathan Confronts King David 21

King David and the Census 27

Ahijah and the Divided Kingdom 34

Shemaiah Confronts Rehoboam 39

Jahaziel Prophesies Deliverance 46

Elijah and the Prophets of Baal 52

Elijah Chooses Elisha 59

Elisha and the Widow 65

Elisha and the Shunammite Woman 74

Obadiah and Edom 80

Joel and the Day of the Lord 90

Jonah Runs Away 98

Amos Calls for Justice 105

Hosea and Gomer 113

The Calling of Isaiah	119
Isaiah and the Coming Messiah	126
Micah's Prophecy: Big News About a Tiny Place	133
Nahum, Ninevah, and Judah	140
Zephaniah and the Restoration of Judah	148
Jeremiah and Jehoiakim	155
Habakkuk Questions God	163
Daniel and the Writing on the Wall	171
Ezekiel and the Dry Bones	179
Haggai and the Rebuilding of the Temple	185
Zechariah and the Temple	192
Malachi Prophesies the Coming Messiah	199
John the Baptist: The Greatest Prophet	207
John the Revelator	214
Now We Take Over	221
Extra Resources	229
How to Lead a Child to Christ	231
How to Become an Excellent Bible Teacher	234
A Note from the Author	239
Coloring Pages	241

INTRODUCTION

Hey! I'm Anne Marie. Thank you for purchasing this book! *What God Is Saying: Object Lessons from the Prophets for Kids* includes 31 interactive object lessons for children ages 5 to 12. These weekly lessons are meant to last 20–30 minutes. I believe the title, *What God Is Saying*, correctly depicts how God used men to share His messages of repentance and hope with the Hebrew people, the Assyrians, the Babylonians, the new Christian church, as well as with us.

This curriculum will help you:

- teach engaging Bible lessons children cannot resist;
- create a fun teaching atmosphere that sparks the imagination of children;
- teach children Biblical truth that enhances their spiritual growth; and
- share the gospel with children and expand the Kingdom.

I am humbled that you have chosen to use this resource! I pray that it will ignite a passion for Jesus in those who hear you teach.

For more resources for parents and teachers, visit https://www.futureflyingsaucers.com/what-god-is-saying-resource-page/.

To receive weekly Bible lessons, book updates, and children's ministry helps, subscribe at https://www.futureflyingsaucers.com/.

Keep on serving the Lord, my friend!

Anne Marie Gosnell
futureflyingsaucers.com

> "For no prophecy was ever produced by the will of man,
> but men spoke from God as they were carried along by the Holy Spirit."
> —2 Peter 1:21 (ESV)

HOW THIS BOOK WORKS

I have put these lessons in an order that encourages spiritual growth. I recommend going in order because they build upon each other. These lessons can be taught with large groups or small groups.

Each lesson has a **free downloadable poster** and other lesson helps that you can access from the **Resources Page** https://www.futureflyingsaucers.com/what-god-is-saying-resource-page/. Discuss and display the posters in the room throughout this series, and read them during each session. You may choose to use the shorter verses as memory verses.

All lessons have a **Background** section. Use this section to help you put the lesson into context, or "set the stage," for the children.

Old Testament history takes place in a variety of locations; therefore, there is a **Geography** section for each lesson. I encourage you to have a map to point out these places. See the Resources Page https://www.futureflyingsaucers.com/what-god-is-saying-resource-page/ for maps.

The **Object Lesson** is usually first and might be referred to throughout the lesson. Most of the objects are items that many children know and see daily. Jesus used common objects such as sheep and trees when He taught, and we can do the same. Preparation time is minimal, and most lessons use materials you will find around your home. I do suggest practicing the lessons ahead of time to be sure you understand how the activity works.

The **Bible Lesson** section is a paraphrase of the event from the **Scripture Focus**. Read the Scripture and the Bible Lesson a few times to prepare for teaching your lesson. Practice enough so you can tell the story without reading.

The last section is essential: **Life Application**. This is where Scripture "comes alive" and the kids learn how to apply it to their lives. If we do not explain the purpose of Scripture to children, then we have failed as Bible teachers. All Scripture is useful, and we must showcase the glorious purpose of the Bible in each lesson.

How This Book Works

At the end of each lesson is a **Comment Box**. This is an area for you to reflect upon your teaching so you can improve your skills. Thinking retrospectively will help you to evaluate your personal ministry. Ask yourself two questions: *"What went well as I taught this lesson?"* and *"What can I do better?"*

For more in-depth Bible teacher training, take a look at my online course, Become an Excellent Bible Teacher (https://futureflyingsaucers-bible-institute.teachable.com/p/excellent-bible-teacher).

I would love to know how your lessons go! Please share your retrospective ideas with me. Also, please leave a book review on the website of your favorite book store. Feel free to contact me at futureflyingsaucers@klopex.com. You can also join my Facebook group, Become an Excellent Bible Teacher: Bible Lessons for Kids (https://www.facebook.com/groups/BibleLessonsForKids/).

A FEW LAST TIPS

■ ■

Encourage the children to use their Bibles. Do not assume they think your story is Biblical just because you tell it. Have them be like the Bereans in the book of Acts (Acts 17:10–12). Show them in the Bible the verses you will be using. Some of the lessons will have the kids either reading along with you or reading for themselves. If you have children who do not read, you can still help them find the reference in the Bible. This is a great habit to start when young.

When you teach a lesson, try not to say words such as, "*Our story today comes from . . .*" While the Bible is the story of God, it is more than a story. We live in a world where the line between fairy tales, fiction, and truth is blurred. Because of this, refer to every person or event as history or biography. Children need to understand that people in Scripture were **real**, breathing people. The places in the Bible were—and some still are—**real** places.

Be enthusiastic when you teach. Do not put on a show, but share the joy of Jesus so that He is contagious! Scripture tells us that if Jesus is lifted up, He will draw all men to Him. Let us lift Him up!

One last thing . . . NEVER be afraid to share your testimony! Someone in the room might need to hear how God has worked in your past, how He is working today, and what He is doing in your future.

1 WHAT IS A PROPHET?

What was a prophet, and why were they so important in the Scriptures? Use this lesson to teach children the purpose of prophets and that Jesus is the ultimate Mediator between people and God.

Scripture Focus: Hebrews 1:1–2, Numbers 12:5–8

Materials:

- Different objects that make sounds (bell, pot with a spoon, shaker, etc.)

Geography: the United Kingdom

Background: God intended to lead His people. In the garden, He walked with Adam and Eve. When God called Abraham, He spoke directly to him. After Moses brought the people out of Egypt, God met them on the mountain. Moses mediated between God and the Hebrews because God did not want the people to perish. From the people's perspective, they very much wanted Moses to speak to them and not God. They were too scared! (Exodus 20:19) Jesus is the ultimate Mediator because He goes between God and all people.

In the past God spoke to our ancestors through the prophets. He spoke to them many times and in many different ways.
—Hebrews 1:1 (ICB)

OBJECT LESSON

[Read Hebrews 1:1–2. Ask:]

- *How many times did God speak?* [various times]
- *Can you think of an example from the Bible when God Himself spoke?* [Allow for answers. Examples could be: at Creation; speaking to Cain, Abraham, and Moses; when Jesus was baptized; etc.]
- *What does the author of Hebrews say is one way that God spoke in the past?* [by the prophets]
- *How does God speak now?* [through His Son, Jesus]

The author of Hebrews tells us that, in the past, God spoke at various times and in various ways to His people. God still speaks to His people. Today He chooses to use the Scriptures and words of His Son Jesus. Because He is God, He can still use various ways and times to speak when He so chooses.

[Bring out the items. Tell the children to listen to the different noises made by the objects. If you like, choose a few student volunteers to play the items. Ask:]

- *What types of sounds did you hear?* [Possible answers: loud, soft, swish-swish, tapping, reverberations, vibrations, etc.]

Our ears are amazing creations. The outside of our ears gathers the vibrations from sounds. As those vibrations travel down the ear canal, eventually they turn into something our brains can understand. Then we are able to discern different sounds: loud and soft sounds, whispering, yelling, a horn blowing, a cat purring, and more!

[Ask:]

- *What are some of your favorite sounds?* [Allow for answers.]

What Is a Prophet?

BIBLE LESSON

In the Old Testament, God chose to speak to people directly, or to use specific people called prophets. There was nothing particularly special about this group of people. They could be men or women. They could be poor or rich, educated or not. What they all had in common was that God had chosen them to send a message to His people. Sometimes the message was for all the people of Israel; sometimes it was for a specific person, like a king. Prophets listened to God and took a message to the correct receiver.

Moses is considered the first prophet.

[Read Numbers 12:5–8. Ask:]

- *Who is speaking in verses 6–8?* [God is speaking to Aaron and Miriam.]
- *How did God make Himself known to a prophet?* [in a vision or a dream]
- *How did God speak with Moses?* [God spoke to him face to face and spoke plainly. Moses saw the form of the Lord.]

When Moses led the Israelites out of Egypt and into the Promised Land, God spoke to him; then Moses would either obey God or give a message to the people. Moses was a mediator. He was in the middle between God and the people. Sometimes the people would come to Moses with messages for God; then Moses would go to God and talk to Him for the people.

A prophet was a mediator.

A prophet was also a leader. Moses physically led the people to the Promised Land. Other prophets would lead the Israelites in different ways. Some would anoint kings. Samuel was the leader of the Hebrews before King Saul. Elijah led the people to confront sin and turn back to God.

[Ask:]

- *Did the people in the Bible have Bibles to read for themselves?* [Yes and no. Historically, people attribute the writing of the first five books of the Bible to Moses. Therefore, anyone who lived before he wrote those books would not have had scrolls or written words of God to read. Throughout the years, more people would write books of history, poetry, or prophecy, and the scribes or leaders would keep the writings. The priests would read the Scriptures to the people, but they did not have their own copies to hold and read like you do today. Even during the time of Jesus, people would go to the temple, or the synagogue, to listen to the Scripture.]

- *If the people did not have a Bible to read, how did they know what God wanted them to do?* [The WORD of the Lord would come to the prophets, and they would speak to the kings or people. The kings and people would need to listen and then obey whatever the prophet said.]

- *Did the kings and people ALWAYS obey the prophets?* [No. See if the children can brainstorm some examples of when the prophets, and therefore God, were disobeyed. Examples: the people refused to go into the Promised Land; during the time of Judges; during the periods of the kings, there were many kings who refused to listen to the prophets, and therefore the people were oppressed or exiled.]

- *Were the prophets ever wrong with the prophecies?* [No, but the prophecies might not have happened during the lifetime of the prophet. For example, one scholar counted 456 prophecies focused on the coming Messiah. Jesus fulfilled 300 of those while here on earth. The others have not taken place yet.]

- *When your parents, caregiver, or other authority figure tells you something important, what do they expect you to do?* [Allow for answers. Hopefully they will say they need to listen and then do whatever is asked of them.]

- *If a pot was hot and you refused to listen to your caregiver tell you the pot was hot, and you touched it, what would happen?* [get burned; have a consequence]

When the prophets spoke, God expected the people to hear them, listen, and obey His words.

Consequences happened when the people or the kings refused to listen to the word of the Lord which was spoken by the prophet. The prophet would give a message or warn the people. Sometimes they would obey the message and other times they would disobey.

LIFE APPLICATION

[Ask:]

- *Do you have a copy of the WORD of the Lord?* [Help the children know that if they have a Bible, then yes, they do. If you notice that one of the children does not have a Bible, then try to give them one, if possible.]
- *Do you need a prophet to tell you the words of God?* [Allow for answers. Explain that we do have prophets to listen to, and their words are recorded in Scripture. Therefore, we should obey what they say. There are also people in the church who are gifted with prophecy as a gift from the Holy Spirit, but we must be careful to make sure that the words from those people match the words in Scripture.]
- *Can we hear God without the Bible?* [Allow for answers.]

Some of the prophets from the Old Testament heard God by using their ears. We can hear from God by listening to Him as well, but we do not usually use our physical ears. We use our heart—not the blood-pumping heart that you have, but what is called your soul-heart, or spirit-heart. Your soul-heart can hear from God, just like your physical ears can hear and discern different sounds. However, in order for your soul-heart to hear well, you need to know God's words from the Bible. It all works together. And when we hear God's words, then we should obey them.

Prophets in the Bible were important because they spoke words from God, led people, and mediated between God and people. Now that we have our own copies of the Bible, we do not need a person to tell us the words of God because we can read those words for ourselves. We should read those words for ourselves! However, there are people such as your preacher, parents, and Sunday School teacher who have listened to God longer than you. They have more practice. You can learn from them about God's Word.

As you listen and read God's Word, the Holy Spirit can speak to your soul-heart and help you figure out what is from God and what is not. We must be willing to listen and obey just like the prophets of old.

What God is Saying

If Jesus is our Savior, then He becomes our mediator between God and us. When we read our Bibles, the Holy Spirit uses those WORDS of God to teach and guide us.

What is God saying through the prophets? God wants to speak to His people. He wants us to listen to Him, take Him seriously, and do what He asks. Sometimes those messages are encouraging. Other times, God warns us about our choices and the consequences of those choices.

What Is a Prophet?

COMMENT BOX

▮▮▮▮▮▮▮▮▮▮▮▮▮▮▮▮▮▮▮▮▮▮

THINK: What went well as you taught this lesson? What can you do better?

_____
_____
_____
_____
_____
_____
_____
_____
_____

TIP: The concept of "listening" to God can be a strange one to children. Discuss with the children what it means to listen to God, hear God, obey God, and follow God.

2 THE CALLING OF SAMUEL

How old does a person have to be for God to use him or her? Use this calling of Samuel lesson to teach that God can use children and people of all ages if they are willing to listen and obey.

Scripture Focus: 1 Samuel 3

Materials:

- One coin
- One die (optional)
- Paper or a whiteboard

Geography: the United Kingdom

Background: The Israelites chose the monarchy form of government because they wanted to be like other nations. Samuel is the prophet chosen by God to lead during this time. In order for a man or woman to be a true prophet of God, the predictive words of the person must be fulfilled. (See Deuteronomy 18:21–22.) When God called to Samuel in the night when he was a boy, this began the establishment of Samuel's credentials as a prophet to all the people of the land.

The Lord was with Samuel as he grew up. He did not let any of Samuel's messages fail to come true.
—1 Samuel 3:19 (ICB)

FUTUREFLYINGSAUCERS.COM

OBJECT LESSON

[Bring out the coin. Ask:]

- *If we flip this coin twenty times, can you predict the number of times it will land on heads (or one particular side)?* [Allow for answers. Write down the predictions.]

[Flip the coin twenty times, and create a tally chart to record the data. Ask:]

- *Were we correct with our prediction of the future?* [If the prediction was very close, have the children predict again, continuing to thirty or forty flips and recording the data. Even if they were close, explain that they were not exactly correct.]

BIBLE LESSON

We have seen how Moses was a prophet of God who was a mediator (someone who stands between). Moses stood between the people of God and God Himself. Some prophets were also leaders of the Israelites. Samuel was both a mediator and a leader, but God also used Samuel to state what was to come in the future. Samuel was a young boy when God began to speak to him.

[Read 1 Samuel 3. Consider assigning volunteers to act out the different roles of Samuel, Eli, and God. Ask:]

- *What do we learn about the word of the Lord at this time of history?* [It was rare; there was no widespread revelation.]
- *When did this event take place?* [when Samuel was a boy; while Eli and Samuel were lying down; before the lamp of God went out in the tabernacle]
- *Who did Samuel think had called him?* [Eli]
- *How many times did God speak to Samuel before Eli figured out what was going on?* [three times]
- *What does God do when He comes to Samuel the fourth time?* [God came, stood, and called.]
- *How did Samuel handle this situation?* [Because Samuel did not know the Lord yet, he wasn't sure what was going on, so he assumed Eli called him. Once Eli guided Samuel and told him how to respond, Samuel obeyed and listened to God.]
- *What emotions do you think Samuel felt?* [Allow for answers. Samuel may have felt confused, anxious, or curious; we are not told how he felt. God does not even tell Samuel not to be afraid. What we do know is that Samuel was afraid to tell God's message to Eli.]
- *What was the message given to Samuel?* [Eli knew his sons were sinful, and he had done nothing to try to guide them back to a righteous life. Because of this, Eli's hereditary line for the high priest would end.]

The Calling of Samuel

Samuel was afraid to tell Eli God's message of what was going to happen. However, Eli wanted to know what message God had given Samuel, so he asked Samuel not to hide the word from him. Samuel obeyed and told Eli God's word. In 1 Samuel 2 we learn that a man of God had already given Eli this exact same prophecy, and Eli had done nothing between the two messages to guide, or discipline, his sons.

LIFE APPLICATION

■ ■ ■ ■ ■ ■ ■ ■ ■ ■ ■ ■ ■ ■ ■ ■ ■ ■ ■

When we flipped the coin, we attempted to predict if it would land on one side or the other. There were only two options. A prophet who had a message from God about the future was different from a coin flip because there are many, many options that can happen in the future. Yet, God's word is always true. What He says will happen. When Samuel received a word from the Lord, and then it happened, that gave Samuel credibility in the eyes of Eli and the Israelites. That meant that Samuel was respected as a true prophet of God, and the people from the northern cities down to the southern cities listened to Samuel even though he was very young.

[Optional: If you have time, do the previous prediction activity again, this time using a six-sided die. Have the children predict which number they think will show up the most after thirty rolls. Roll the die thirty times and tally the data. Discuss how many options there were this time for dice rolls versus the coin toss (six options versus two). Ask:]

- *What are some ways people try to predict the future today?* [Possible answers may include weather prediction, economic trends, or societal trends.]
- *How good are people at knowing the future?* [Sometimes weather predictions and others are correct because they use scientific laws or trends to predict what might happen. However, there will always be a percentage of error.]
- *What happened when prophets spoke a message from God about the future?* [Everything they said came true just as God said it would.]
- *Have all prophecies from the Bible happened?* [not yet]
- *Do we still have prophets today?* [Some scholars consider John the Baptist as the last of the Old Covenant prophets because he spoke just before Jesus started His ministry. Jesus is considered the last true prophet because He was God and spoke for the Father and Himself.]

- *Do you need a prophet to tell you the words of God?* [Allow for answers. Explain that we do have prophets to listen to, and their words are recorded in Scripture; there are also people in the church who are gifted with prophecy, but we must be careful to make sure that the words from those people match the words in Scripture. (Deut. 18:21–22)]

Prophets in the Bible were important because they spoke words from God, led people, and mediated between God and people. Now that we have our own copies of the Bible, we do not really need an actual PERSON to tell us the words of God because we can read those words for ourselves. And we should.

Sometimes prophecies did not happen for many years, sometimes hundreds of years. Examples of this would be prophecies about Jesus. Bible scholars think that there are more than 400 prophecies about Jesus in the Old Testament, and He fulfilled at least 300 while on Earth.

God used Samuel in mighty ways all throughout his lifetime, from his young days until he was very old. He anointed the first two kings of Israel, and he spoke God's word to the people as he traveled throughout the land.

What is God saying through Samuel? God wants to speak to you through His word while you are young and all throughout your life. He wants to do mighty things with you just like He did with Samuel. Are you willing to say, *"Yes, your servant is listening"*?

What God is Saying

COMMENT BOX

■ ■ ■ ■ ■ ■ ■ ■ ■ ■ ■ ■ ■ ■ ■ ■ ■ ■ ■

THINK: What went well as you taught this lesson? What can you do better?

_____
_____
_____
_____
_____
_____
_____
_____
_____

TIP: Consider giving your children age-appropriate Bible reading logs and rewarding them each week for their Bible reading. You can find some Bible reading logs on the Resource Page.

3 NATHAN CONFRONTS KING DAVID

The prophet Nathan called out King David for his sin against Bathsheba and the murder of her husband, Uriah. Use this object lesson to teach children that God sees our sin and desires for us to repent.

Scripture Focus: 2 Samuel 12:7, 11:1–12:15

Materials:

- A ring or piece of jewelry (or another item) that is important or sentimental to you
- Picture of the crown jewels or other royal jewelry (see Resource Page)

Geography: Jerusalem, about 1000 B.C.

Background: Nathan prophesied during the reigns of King David and King Solomon. He was a court prophet, offering counsel to kings. He appeared in Biblical accounts four times. In this event, God sent him to confront David over his sin with Bathsheba and his murder of her husband, Uriah.

Then Nathan said to David, "You are the man!" —2 Samuel 12:7 (ICB)

OBJECT LESSON

[Show your ring or special item to the children. Describe how much you like the item, who gave it to you, and why it is special. Tell a similar story to the one below.]

Take a look at my ring. It is one of my very favorite things because my husband gave it to me. He spent a lot of time looking for this and saving up for it because he wanted to show me that he loved me. I love this ring SO very much because it reminds me of how much my husband loves me every time I look at it.

Let's pretend! I want us to pretend that I went all the way over to another nation to visit some friends.

While I was there, I got the once-in-a-lifetime chance to meet the monarch of the country! Can you imagine how excited I was? I got dressed up in my finest clothes, and, of course, I wore my beautiful ring.

When I met the monarch, he noticed my sparkly, wonderful ring and remarked that it was very beautiful. I told him my husband gave it to me. Later that night, a representative from the monarch came to my hotel. He said that the monarch admired my ring so very much, and he wanted to add it to his collection of all his many crown jewels. Of course, I said, *"No, my husband gave me this!"* I could not part with it. The representative tried to talk me into giving my ring to the king, but I would not do it.

The next morning, soldiers from the king came and took me to prison. They took my ring away and gave it to the king.

[Show the picture of the crown jewels. Discuss what is seen and the richness of the items. Compare them to your special ring or item. Ask:]

- *Would it be fair for the king/queen, who has all of these special riches, to take my one special thing?* [no]
- *How would you feel if something like that happened to you?* [Allow for answers.]

Many monarchs are known worldwide for their famous collections of jewels. It would not be right for them to take my ring when they have all those others.

BIBLE LESSON

Nathan the prophet prophesied about 1,000 years before Jesus was born. Nathan was a prophet during the reign of King David, and then during the reign of David's son, King Solomon.

Back in those days, kings used to go out and wage wars against each other in the spring. Scripture says it was time for kings to go to war, but David stayed home in Jerusalem and sent his commander, Joab, to lead instead. This was King David's first mistake.

One night while he was in his palace, he could not sleep and went out on the rooftop. He saw down below him on a housetop a lady taking a bath. She was very beautiful, and King David decided he wanted her to be his.

He asked someone who this lady was, and found out her name was Bathsheba. She was a married lady, the wife of his own soldier, Uriah. He sent people to go and bring her to him.

Bathsheba came to King David that night. David thought she was so lovely and treated her like she was one of his many wives. But remember, she was already married. Later, Bathsheba sent word to him that she was pregnant with David's baby. David decided to trick Uriah, and when that did not work he plotted to get rid of him.

David told his commander, Joab, to send Bathsheba's husband, Uriah, into the part of the battle where the fighting was the fiercest, and then to pull back all the defenders so that Uriah would be killed. David actually had Bathsheba's husband murdered!

[Read 2 Samuel 12:1–9, 13–14. Ask:]

- *How did Nathan communicate the truth to King David?* [He used the story of a lamb being taken from a poor man by a rich man.]
- *How did David respond to Nathan's story?* [He was angry and wanted to punish the man with death.]
- *Who was the rich man Nathan was talking about in his object lesson about the little lamb?* [David]

- *How did David respond after realizing he was the rich man?* [David recognized his sin and admitted it.]

Nathan brought a message from God to David. This was God speaking to David about how He hated what David had done. David had everything; God had made him king and given him anything he desired. However, David still took Uriah's wife. David made many mistakes. He sinned.

Nathan had to show David how God saw David taking Uriah's wife and having him killed. God was displeased. After Nathan brought him this message from God, David, who was called *"a man after God's own heart,"* realized what he had done. He said, *"I have sinned against the Lord."* He knew that when we sin against people, we sin against God.

Nathan said, *"The Lord has taken away your sin."* That must have been good news to David! God forgave him. However, sin always has consequences. Since David had shown what Nathan called *"utter contempt for the Lord,"* the baby born from King David and Bathsheba died.

[Ask:]

- *Do you think Nathan wanted to bring these messages to the king?* [Probably not. He knew that the king could have him arrested or even killed.]
- *Why did Nathan go to King David?* [According to verse 1, God sent Nathan to tell David about his sin. Nathan obeyed God.]

God gave Nathan the message, so he knew it had to be true. Nathan knew that he had to go before the king and call him out for what he had done. Thankfully, David realized his sin and took the blame for his mistakes.

LIFE APPLICATION

[Ask:]

- *Raise your hand if you have made a mistake.* [Raise your own hand. Discuss why everyone should have their hand raised. We all make mistakes, and usually they do not hurt anyone. For example, burning a piece of toast is a mistake.]
- *Raise your hand if you have ever sinned against someone else; for instance, hitting your sister, lying, thinking jealous thoughts, being rude to your mom or caregiver, making fun of a kid at school.* [Raise your hand. Again, everyone should have their hand raised, because we all sin against each other. Sometimes sin is unintentional. We hurt someone and do not mean to. Other times we purposefully hurt people.]
- *Did you have a consequence for your sin?* [Allow for answers. If anyone says that they did not receive a consequence, discuss how sometimes consequences do not come right away. Also, discuss how God sees what we do even if no one else does.]
- *Who is the only person who never sinned against anyone?* [Jesus]

Jesus came and lived His whole life without sin. He then went to the cross and died for us and rose again so that we would be forgiven for our sins. Nathan told David that God had put away, or forgiven, his sin because David was totally sorry for what he had done.

When we confess our sins, God is faithful and just to forgive us our sins, too. I am so glad we don't have to carry the weight of all the wrong things we have done.

What was God saying through Nathan? David had sinned. God showed David how he had not only sinned against Bathsheba, Uriah, and the soldiers, but against God Himself. We can go to God, too, just like David, and repent—turn back—from the wrong things we have done. We can count on God to forgive us.

COMMENT BOX

THINK: What went well as you taught this lesson? What can you do better?

_____
_____
_____
_____
_____
_____
_____
_____
_____
_____

TIP: The event of David and Bathsheba has some content that is not age-appropriate for younger children. Know your children well enough to know what they can handle.

4 KING DAVID AND THE CENSUS

Use this lesson about King David and the census to teach the horridness of sin, the goodness of confession, and the importance of sacrifice.

Scripture Focus: 2 Samuel 24 (cross reference with 1 Chronicles 21)

Materials:

- A container of coins—at least a few hundred

Geography: Israel, Judah, Jerusalem, the temple mount

Background: It is important to remember that all of the Old Testament is the story of God creating a nation from which His Son, the Savior of the world, would come. God's promise to Abraham was four-fold: 1) He would give land. 2) He would make a great nation. 3) He would make Abraham's name great. 4) All the people of the world would be blessed through this nation.

It is important to note that in Exodus 30:11–12, God gives directions for how to go about a census. Each person counted was to give a ransom, or a sum of money, to the Lord. This money would have gone to the tabernacle. This ransom was to be given so a plague did not come upon the people.

The Lord told Gad,
"Go and tell David,
'This is what the Lord says:
I offer you three choices.
Choose one for me to do to you.'"
—2 Samuel 24:12 (ICB)

Kings would take a census for different reasons. The main one would be to see how many men would be available to form an army.

OBJECT LESSON

[Show the container of coins. Say:]

I want to know how many coins I have in this container.

[Split the children into pairs. Give each group a handful of coins. Lead them to put the coins into stacks of ten to make them easy to count. Act pridefully about the coins as the children are counting. Feel free to laugh maniacally, use body language that shows pride, and say things such as, *"I can't wait to see how many coins I have! I will have the most coins of everyone!"* Have fun with this! Be sure to count COINS, not the money amount. Get a total count of the coins. Say:]

Yes! I always wanted to know how many coins I had in that container, and now I know.

[Ask:]

- *What should I do with these coins?* [Allow for answers. As the children give answers, shake your head no to anything that is giving to others, and act pridefully towards any ideas that give you something. Really be over the top. An example to say would be, *"Why should I give my coins to help so-and-so, or do that?"* Make it obvious that you think you are the best because of these coins. See if you can get the children disgusted with your attitude.]

[Stop acting and ask:]

- *What is wrong with what I am doing?* [Allow for answers. Lead the children to discuss pride and greed.]
- *Is there anything wrong with counting coins?* [no]
- *What was wrong with the way I was going about counting the coins?* [Allow for answers. Help children to see that the motivation for counting the coins makes the difference.]

King David and the Census

BIBLE LESSON

King David did something that we would think was harmless, but God did not like David's motivation, and the consequences were extreme.

[Read 2 Samuel 24:1–4. Ask:]

- *What did King David want to do?* [count the number of people in his kingdom]
- *Where did David get the idea?* [Verse 1 tells us that the Lord was angry with Israel. In 1 Chronicles it says that Satan stood against Israel and moved David to take the census. Whether Satan gave David the idea or David came up with it himself does not matter. God allowed David to make this choice.]
- *Who argued with King David about the census?* [Joab]
- *Why do you think Joab spoke against King David's decision?* [Joab must have known the Scripture from Exodus where God gives directions for taking a census. He knew that King David was not taking the ransom that God desired. It could be that Joab, a long-time friend and advisor to King David, noticed that King David's motivation was prideful or selfish.]

Even though Joab thought the census was a bad idea, he obeyed the king anyway. He and the commanders of the army traveled counterclockwise through the land registering, or counting, the people. Scripture tells us that they brought back numbers revealing the number of men able to fight in a war. It is possible King David wanted to know how mighty his kingdom was without thinking about God's protection of the kingdom.

[Read 2 Samuel 24:10–14. Ask:]

- *How did David feel?* [His heart troubled him.]
- *What did David do?* [He confessed his sin to God, asked for forgiveness, and agreed that he had been foolish.]
- *Who was Gad?* [David's seer, a prophet of God]

- *What did God tell Gad?* [He was to go speak to King David. God was giving David three choices as a consequence for the census. David was to choose between three years of famine in the land, three months of fleeing from foes, or three days of pestilence, or plague, in the land.]
- *What choice does King David make?* [He desired to fall into the hands of the Lord and not into the hands of man, so he chose three days of plague.]
- *Why does David want God and not man?* [David acknowledges that God is filled with mercy. Men might not be.]

[Read 2 Samuel:15–18. Ask:]

- *How many men died?* [70,000]

We learn about an angel in this Scripture. The angel was striking down the people with plague and was about to destroy Jerusalem.

Then God was moved with compassion and stopped the angel from destroying any more.

[Ask:]

- *What was David's reaction?* [David realized he was the one who had done wrong and sinned. His people had not. They were innocent in this situation.]
- *What does Gad tell David to do?* [make an altar on a threshing floor]

David went to the place where Gad told him to go. The threshing floor was owned by one of David's people. The man offered the land to David and even the cattle to sacrifice. However, King David did not want to take something for nothing. He knew that he needed to pay. This altar needed to cost him something.

Therefore, David paid the owner for the threshing floor, the land around the floor, and the wood and cattle for the offerings.

[Ask:]

- *Why do you think this particular threshing floor was so important?* [Allow for answers. This is where the angel was standing when God told it to stop the plague. This would be the place where Solomon would build the temple. Bible scholars also think this is the place where Abraham offered Isaac as a sacrifice.]

LIFE APPLICATION

[Show the coins. Ask and discuss:]

- *What was my motivation for having you count these coins?* [Allow for answers, which may include selfishness, pride, or greed.]
- *How does this event with King David prove to us that God knows the motivations of our hearts?* [Allow for answers. Scripture does not tell us, but there seems to be no dialogue between David and God before David made the decision to count the people. There is, however, prayer and lamenting after David realized the wrong he had done. Read Jeremiah 17:10 and discuss.]
- *As a consequence of his actions, what did Gad say David needed to do?* [David was to build an altar. Read 2 Samuel 24:25. Explain that David had to offer sacrifices (burnt offerings and peace offerings) for his sin.]

God takes sin seriously. It does not seem like a big deal to us to count the number of soldiers in a kingdom, but God knew David's motivation, and He was not pleased with it. In fact, we know from verse 1 that God was angry with Israel, and He used King David to bring about a judgment. This may seem strange to us, but sometimes God tests us. James 1:13 tells us that God is not responsible for sin. And Psalm 18:30 tells us that God's ways are perfect. We just do not always understand God's ways.

Seventy thousand people died because of King David's choice to sin. Sin demands death and punishment. Sacrifice is a solution. It demands blood. King David knew that, which is why he had to pay for the threshing floor land and not take it for free.

[Ask:]

- *Have you ever done something wrong and other people were hurt in the process?* [Allow for answers. Give an example from your own life.]

It would be nice if only the person who sinned was hurt by the sin. That is not how it works. Our sin affects others.

Your sin demands punishment. Your sin demands sacrifice and blood. We do not build an altar and kill cows on it, though. Instead, we look to Jesus. It is His blood that was sacrificed for the wrongs you have done and will do.

God knows your heart. He knows why you do the things you do. He knows when you are greedy, prideful, or selfish, or when you think mean thoughts about someone else. God sent Jesus to die on the cross for you.

Jesus' sacrifice was costly.

[Hold up the coins.]

No number of coins in the world can pay for your sins. Only Jesus can do that.

What is God saying through King David and Gad the prophet? David had to confess that what he did was wrong. Then he was told to offer sacrifices to make things right with God. You can do the same. Confess your sin to God, and make things right with Him by believing Jesus died for you.

COMMENT BOX

THINK: What went well as you taught this lesson? What can you do better?

_____
_____
_____
_____
_____
_____
_____
_____
_____
_____

TIP: It is hard for people to understand the mind of God, and there are some events in Scripture that can be disturbing. Remind children that it is ok to have questions without answers, and that God's ways are not our ways.

5 AHIJAH AND THE DIVIDED KINGDOM

Use this lesson about Ahijah, Jeroboam, and the divided kingdom to teach that God desires to bless those who choose Him.

Scripture Focus: 1 Kings 11:28–38

Materials:

- Large flat sheet (use an old one, preferably one with stripes, or one that looks "cloak-like")
- Scissors

Geography: Jerusalem, Israel; 940–915 B.C.

Background: Solomon was on the throne of Israel. Unfortunately, he did not heed God's warnings and married many women who worshipped idols. To please his wives and concubines, Solomon built altars and worship areas on the high places around Israel and Jerusalem. Idolatrous and immoral actions, including the sacrifices of children, took place at the high places. God became angry.

Preparation: You will be ripping the sheet into twelve sections. Take scissors and clip eleven short snips into the sheet fabric so you can rip the pieces more easily.

One day Jeroboam was leaving Jerusalem. Ahijah, the prophet from Shiloh, met him on the road. Ahijah was wearing a new coat. The two men were alone out in the country.
—1 Kings 11:29 (ICB)

OBJECT AND BIBLE LESSON

[Drape the sheet over your shoulders and wear it like a cloak. Say:]

When Solomon became King of Israel, his heart seemed to belonged to God. When God appeared to Solomon, Solomon humbly asked God for wisdom. That pleased God.

Over the years, Solomon made many political marriages; he also had many women in his home to whom he was not married, but acted like he was. Many of these women brought their idols with them.

Consequently, Solomon tried to worship God AND man-made idols.

God was not happy. In 1 Kings 11:11, God told Solomon that He was going to take away the kingdom and give it to a servant. Because of God's love for King David, Solomon's father, God would not take away the kingdom from Solomon, but from Solomon's son.

[Read 1 Kings 11:28–38. Ask:]

- *What do we learn about Jeroboam in verse 28?* [He was a valiant warrior; Solomon noticed him because he was industrious; Solomon placed Jeroboam in charge of all the slaves and forced labor. The *"house of Joseph"* means the tribes of Ephraim and Manasseh.]
- *Who did Jeroboam meet, and where were they?* [Ahijah the Shilonite; outside the city of Jerusalem, on a road, in a field]
- *What did Ahijah do?* [Ahijah had on a new cloak, and he tore it into twelve pieces.]

[Take the "cloak" off of your shoulders. Rip the sheet into twelve pieces. Do not say anything as you rip. Allow the children to react to you.]

After Ahijah ripped his new cloak, he let Jeroboam choose ten pieces. He also told Jeroboam what God wanted him to know.

[Count out ten pieces. Hold the pieces in one hand up so the children can see them.]

Because of the sins of King Solomon, God was going to tear ten of the twelve tribes away from Solomon's line of kings.

[Put the other two pieces in the other hand and hold those up.]

The tribe of Judah would stay with Solomon's family. The tribe of Judah had pulled in the tribe of Benjamin over the years. That is why Judah was considered as two tribes left for Solomon.

Through the prophet Ahijah, God told Jeroboam that he would rip ten tribes from Solomon's son.

[Ask:]

- *What promises does God give Jeroboam in verse 38?* [If Jeroboam listened to God's commands and did what was right in God's sight, then God would be with him and create an enduring kingdom for him.]

LIFE APPLICATION

What an amazing blessing that is! God gave Jeroboam a conditional promise. IF Jeroboam followed God's commands and did what was right when he was king, THEN God would be with him and give Jeroboam an enduring kingdom.

God wants to bless us. There are blessings God gives us that He freely gives, like salvation. There are other times when God wants to bless us when we walk in His ways and do what is right.

However, sometimes we choose to go our own way. That's what Jeroboam eventually did. Jeroboam did become king over ten tribes just as Ahijah had said. However, Jeroboam chose to build worship areas to God and other gods on the high places, and he did not walk in the ways of God.

[Ask:]

- *Do you think God gave Jeroboam the blessings He offered?* [no]

Jeroboam missed out on amazing blessings from God because he chose to ignore God's commands and not walk in the ways of God.

Jeroboam's kingdom became the northern nation of Israel, while the other two tribes became the southern nation of Judah. Jeroboam and all of the kings who came after him chose to rebel against God. Because of that, when the time was right, God used the Assyrian Empire to take over the nation of Israel and scatter the people throughout the lands.

[Ask:]

- *Have you ever been in a situation where you chose to rebel against a caregiver's and God's ways, and then you missed out on possible blessings?* [Allow for answers. Help the children realize that most times we do not ever know which blessings we miss because of sin. This is one reason why walking in the ways of God can be motivating. God WANTS to bless those who walk in His ways.]

What is God saying through Ahijah? There are consequences when we choose to live a life against God. There are blessings when we choose to live a life with God. Which will you choose?

COMMENT BOX

THINK: What went well as you taught this lesson? What can you do better?

_____
_____
_____
_____
_____
_____
_____
_____
_____
_____

TIP: Help the children understand the meaning of the word "repentance." Many prophets called the people of Israel to repent. Repentance is more than being sorry for something. It means to change totally, or transform, everything we think, say, and do so we can stay away from what is wrong. We can only do this in the power of the Holy Spirit.

6 SHEMAIAH CONFRONTS REHOBOAM

Shemaiah had to give Rehoboam, the king of Judah, and all his leaders the word that God had abandoned them due to the unfaithfulness of Judah. Use this lesson to teach about heart change, repentance, and salvation.

Scripture Focus: 2 Chronicles 12:1–12

Materials:

- Bag of chocolate chips
- Silicone candy mold
- Microwave-safe bowl
- Spoon to stir chocolate after melting
- A way to melt the chocolate chips (double boiler or microwave)
- Small pitcher with spout (like a cream pitcher) to pour chocolate into molds
- Oven mitts to move bowl of melted chocolate
- Bowl of ice or refrigerator to cool the chocolate (optional)

Geography: Southern Kingdom of Judah and Egypt, around 920 B.C.

Then Shemaiah the prophet came to Rehoboam and the leaders of Judah. They had gathered in Jerusalem because they were afraid of Shishak.
—2 Chronicles 12:5 (ICB)

Background: Shemaiah prophesied during the reign of Rehoboam, the son of Solomon, at the beginning of the divided kingdoms. He also wrote a book of the chronicles of Rehoboam's reign (2 Chronicles 12:15). The people of Judah had *"followed in the ways of David and Solomon"* in the first three years of Rehoboam's reign. However, after Rehoboam became strong, he, the leaders, and the people abandoned God.

It is important to note that this account is the first time an Egyptian king is mentioned by name. Up to this point in Scripture, the leaders were always referred to as *"Pharoah."* King Shishak of Egypt, who reigned from 945–924 B.C., was also known as Sheshonk I. He was from Libyan descent, and there is archeological evidence of his existence and of his conquering parts of Israel and Judah.

Shemaiah Confronts Rehoboam

OBJECT AND BIBLE LESSON

[Show the packet of chocolate chips. Ask:]

- *Who likes chocolate chips?* [Allow for answers and build excitement.]

We are going to do a science experiment with these chocolate chips. We are going to change their form, not once, but twice!

The prophet Shemaiah had to stand up and confront King Rehoboam and all his leaders. It must have been scary to do that, because the king had the power of life and death over people in those days. But God had given Shemaiah a message, and he counted on God to be with him as he carried out the task.

[Pour the chocolate chips into the microwave-safe bowl. Read 2 Chronicles 12:1–12.]

- *When did Rehoboam forsake the law of the Lord?* [after he had established himself and was strong]
- *Who came against Jerusalem?* [Shishak, king of Egypt]
- *Why did he come against Jerusalem?* [because the people of Judah had sinned against the Lord]
- *Why do you think all of the leaders of Judah were in Jerusalem?* [King Shishak had taken all of the other fortified cities of Judah, and it is possible the leaders were hiding themselves in the safety of Jerusalem.]
- *What was Shemaiah's message to the leaders?* [Because you have forsaken or forgotten God, He is going to leave you in the hands of Shishak.]
- *How do you think Shemaiah felt when he told the king and the leaders that God was going to abandon them and let King Shishak and the Egyptians destroy them?* [Allow for answers.]
- *How did King Rehoboam and the leaders respond?* [They humbled themselves before the Lord and said He was righteous.]

- *Why did Shishak not treat Jerusalem the way he did the other fortified cities?* [God responded and gave Shemaiah a new word. He said that He would not destroy Jerusalem, but that Shishak would make them his servants.]
- *What did Shishak do?* [He took away the treasures of the temple and the king's house, even the gold shields of Solomon.]
- *What lesson do you think Rehoboam learned?* [Point out verse 12. It was because of humility that Jerusalem and the kingdom were not totally destroyed.]

[Show the chocolate chips. Say:]

These chocolate chips represent the people of Judah and their king and leaders. When we melt them, it is like Shemaiah's message from God saying He was going to destroy the people of Judah because of their sin.

[Melt the chocolates. Allow children to observe, keeping a safe distance. When melted, stir the chocolate. Then carefully spoon the chocolate into a pitcher with a spout. Say:]

This is what should have happened to the king and people of Judah. God said He was going to destroy them. We destroyed the chocolate chips.

Something unexpected happened! The king, together with his rulers, humbled themselves. That means they realized that God alone is in charge. He alone is worthy of their worship. They recognized they had done wrong in not following God's law, and had led the people of Judah into doing wrong.

God then changed what He was doing. He **was** going to remove His protection from Judah and allow Shishak to destroy the place and the people. When the king and leaders responded with humility, acknowledging God's righteousness and justice, God did not allow Shishak to totally destroy Judah.

[Show the melted chocolate chips. Ask:]

- *Can we change the chocolate chips?* [Allow for answers.]

[Carefully pour chocolate from the pitcher into the chocolate molds. Let the children watch you do it. Depending on the age/ability of the children, you could allow them to help pour. Once the molds are filled, carefully put them in the refrigerator or onto a bowl of ice.]

BIBLICAL APPLICATION

God rewarded the heart change in King Rehoboam and his leaders by changing the outcome of the battle. This is called a reversible change, because God changed what He was doing.

[Reread 2 Chronicles 12:9–12. Ask:]

- *What shields did Shishak take?* [the gold shields Solomon had made]
- *How did Rehoboam replace them?* [He had bronze shields made. Explain that bronze was pretty and shiny like gold, but it was not nearly as precious or expensive. The imitations were not as nice as the originals.]
- *Who took care of the shields?* [They were given to the captains of the guards of the king's house. It was their job to bring out the shields whenever the king entered the house of the Lord.]
- *When would the king see these shields?* [whenever he entered the house of the Lord]
- *Why do you think he had the guards do that?* [Allow for answers. Perhaps Rehoboam used those shields as a reminder of what God did for him and to keep him humble. Read verse 12 again.]

Rehoboam and the leaders deserved God's wrath, but instead they turned from their sin. You have sinned against God and deserve His wrath as well. BUT! When you turn away from your sin, and turn from your ways to following God's ways, this shows the change in your heart. You can make a reversible change.

God sees your reversible change and makes it irreversible. That means it cannot be changed back. When you belong to Jesus, you belong to Him forever and you cannot go back to your old self! That is good news! That means God will never change His mind about you—He sees you as His child.

[Check on the chocolates. If not fully hardened yet, show them how the chocolate is no longer liquid, but changing form. If they are hardened enough, pop one out of the mold and show it to them. Say:]

The chocolate is now hardened back into solid chocolate. The change was reversed! Rehoboam and the leaders deserved to be destroyed because of their sin. We deserve to the destroyed because of our sin. Rehoboam chose God's way and reversed the situation. You can, too.

[Ask:]

- *Can you think of a way that this chocolate could be irreversibly changed—changed in a way that it cannot be changed back to solid chocolate?* [Allow for answers. Explain that if the chocolate were grated and baked into a cake with other ingredients, that would be an irreversible change. Or if the chocolate were ground into powder, added to milk and sugar, and heated, that would make hot chocolate—an irreversible change.]

What is God saying through Shemaiah and Rehoboam? God allows us to change. We can change from not following Him to choosing to follow Jesus. That reversible change is repentance. The irreversible change from God is salvation from sin.

Shemaiah Confronts Rehoboam

COMMENT BOX

■ ■ ■ ■ ■ ■ ■ ■ ■ ■ ■ ■ ■ ■ ■ ■ ■ ■ ■ ■

THINK: What went well as you taught this lesson? What can you do better?

_____
_____
_____
_____
_____
_____
_____
_____
_____

TIP: If you are teaching in a shorter amount of time, prepare some molded chocolate ahead of time. You could have a piece for each child! Yum!

7 JAHAZIEL PROPHESIES DELIVERANCE

King Jehoshaphat and the people of Judah were told that armies from three different nations were coming together to attack them. Use this lesson to teach how God gives directions and protection to His people.

Scripture Focus: 2 Chronicles 20:1–30

Materials:

- A clear glass
- Paper towels
- Clear container (or bowl) of water

Geography: Southern Kingdom of Judah in the area of En Gedi, approximately 870–850 B.C.

Background: King Jehoshaphat was the king of the Southern Kingdom of Judah. In 2 Chronicles 19, we learn that Jehoshaphat set up an extensive legal system across the kingdom. His directions were to fear the Lord in all decisions. Jehoshaphat tried to do what was right in the sight of the Lord.

Jahaziel was a Levite and a worship leader. Jahaziel was given a prophecy through the Spirit of God during the reign of Jehoshaphat.

Then the Spirit of the Lord entered Jahaziel.
—2 Chronicles 20:14 (ICB)

OBJECT AND BIBLE LESSON

[Show the container with water, the glass, and the paper towels. Ask:]

- *Can you think of a way we can submerge the paper towels in the water and NOT get them wet?* [Allow for answers, no matter how crazy they may be. Maybe try a few of the ideas that you know will not work.]

We have a problem we need to solve. We want to put the paper towel into the water, but we do not want it to get wet.

King Jehoshaphat had a problem as well—a big problem. Jehoshaphat was a king who did what was right before the Lord. He is a good role model, or example, for us.

[Read 2 Chronicles 20:1–13. Ask:]

- *Who came to battle against Jehoshaphat?* [the people of Moab and Ammon, and others]
- *How did Jehoshaphat react?* [He was fearful, but he sought the Lord. He had all the people fast and gathered people together to ask the Lord for help.]
- *What do we learn about God through Jehoshaphat's prayer?* [Allow for answers. Lead them to see that the king acknowledged that God rules over all the nations; power and might belong to the Lord; God will hear and save.]
- *What do we learn about the king and the people of Judah through his prayer?* [Allow for answers. Lead them to see that Jehoshaphat claimed they had no power over the armies; they did not know what to do, but they were watching and waiting on God.]
- *Who stood before the Lord?* [all of Judah including men, women, and children]

[Show the bowl of water.]

Jehoshaphat had a problem. Right now, we do as well. Our problem is not nearly as important and dangerous as the king's, but we still need to have a solution.

[Place the paper towel inside the glass.]

One solution for us is to place the towel inside the glass before putting the glass straight into the water.

[Ask:]

- *Do you think my solution will work?* [Allow for answers.]

We will wait and see. The people are waiting to see what God is going to do. They believe He will do something; they just do not know what.

[Read 2 Chronicles 20:14–30. Be excited and dramatic when you read. Ask:]

- *Who spoke?* [a Levite named Jahaziel]
- *What was the first part of his message from God?* [Do not be afraid. The battle belongs to the Lord.]
- *What directions did God give the king through Jahaziel?* [Go down to the armies. Position yourselves, be still, and see the salvation of the Lord.]
- *How did the king react?* [He bowed his face to the ground and worshipped the Lord. All of Judah followed him.]
- *What did the Levites do?* [They stood to praise the Lord with loud voices.]
- *What did the people do as they were going down to meet the armies?* [They sang and praised God!]
- *What did God do while the people were singing?* [He caused the enemy armies to rise up and destroy each other.]
- *Why were the people able to take so much spoil and valuables?* [Conquering armies would strip the dead bodies of anything of value to take back to their own country. Because all of the enemy soldiers were slain, the people of Judah were able to walk right in and take the spoil. It took three days to collect it all. Those were some LARGE armies!]
- *What happened on the fourth day?* [The people gathered to bless the Lord.]

- *Why did the kingdom of Jehoshaphat become quiet?* [The fear of God was upon all of the countries that surrounded Judah.]

God's message through Jahaziel was one of direction and protection. God told the king what to do, and the king obeyed.

[Pick up the glass with the paper towel in it. Be sure the paper towel is balled up in the bottom of the glass so that it does not fall out when you turn it over. Make sure no paper sticks outside the glass. Hold the glass straight, opening down, and put it quickly straight down to the bottom of the container. Then carefully pull the glass out, straight up. If done correctly, the paper towel should be dry. Explain all of these directions as you complete the experiment. *Be sure to practice this with the EXACT items you will be using to present the lesson.*]

The paper towel is dry! We followed the directions, and the paper towel was protected.

BIBLE APPLICATION

Our paper towel was protected, just like God's people.

[Ask:]

- *Can you think of a time when you realized God had protected you or a family member from something?* [Allow for answers.]
- *Is there a prayer request you have for God?* [Allow for answers. Write down the prayer requests and make a point to revisit them next lesson to see if any have been answered. Discuss how God answered the request. Sometimes He does something unexpected.]

God keeps His promises and protects His people. That does not mean nothing bad ever happens to us. We live in a fallen world as sinners, surrounded by people who are sinners. But God promises He uses whatever we go through in life for our good and His glory.

What is God saying through Jahaziel and King Jehoshaphat? Go to God when you are scared. Believe God will do something. Watch for God, praise Him, and just like the people of Judah, you will see a victory.

COMMENT BOX

THINK: What went well as you taught this lesson? What can you do better?

_____
_____
_____
_____
_____
_____
_____
_____
_____

TIP: Start and end the lesson with worship music.

8 ELIJAH AND THE PROPHETS OF BAAL

■■■■■■■■■■■■■■■■■■■

Bible lessons can be fun and interactive, but still teach important concepts. Use this object lesson experience to teach children the power of the one true God.

Scripture Focus: 1 Kings 18:19–40

Materials:

- Two plastic rectangular tablecloths (one red, one yellow)
- Backdrop (a large refrigerator box or a photography backdrop)
- Tape
- An adult to hide behind the backdrop
- Child volunteers to help act out the story (If you have a small group, reuse volunteers.)

Geography: Israel, Samaria, Mount Carmel

Background: King Ahab and his wife Jezebel were evil leaders of the kingdom of Israel. Jezebel promoted her worship of Baal around the nation. Elijah, whose name means "Yahweh is my God," would be a thorn in Ahab's side. God gave Elijah a mission, and it focused on demonstrating to all of Israel who really was the one true God.

"Lord, answer my prayer.
Show these people that you, Lord, are God.
Then the people will know that you are
bringing them back to you."
—1 Kings 18:37 (ICB)

Elijah and the Prophets of Baal

Preparation:

1. Unfold the tablecloths from the packages.
2. Refold them length-wise two times.
3. Cut the table cloths, length-wise, from the bottom, into 4-inch to 5-inch strips, but do not cut all the way to the top. Leave about 6–7 inches uncut.
4. Place the tablecloths on top of each other with the uncut areas on top of each other.
5. All of the strips should be in the same direction.
6. Fan fold, or mountain fold, the uncut portion of the table cloths across the width. Bundle it slightly and use the tape to create a handle. This is your "fire" from heaven.

Place the backdrop so the children will sit in front of it. Have your helper hide behind the backdrop so the children cannot see him. Tell your helper that when you say, *"And after Elijah prayed, FIRE came down from heaven,"* he is then to flip the strips of "fire" over the backdrop.

OBJECT AND BIBLE LESSON

[Direct the children to cheer when they hear the name of Elijah. Be sure to tell them to have self-control while they do this, or they will have to stop. Tell the story of 1 Kings 18:19–40.]

There was a famine in the land of Israel. King Ahab and Queen Jezebel ruled. Because of Queen Jezebel, the worship of Baal was common among the people.

The Lord told Elijah [YEA!] to tell King Ahab to gather all of the people of Israel at Mount Carmel. Not only was King Ahab to gather the people, but he was also to gather 450 prophets of Baal and 400 other prophets that ate at Jezebel's table.

Ahab did as he was told. All of the people and the prophets went to Mount Carmel to see Elijah [YEA!].

Elijah [YEA!] asked the people, *"How long are you going to choose both idols and the one true God? If you are going to follow God, then follow Him. If you are going to follow idols, then follow them."*

The people were silent.

Elijah [YEA!] cried out, *"I am one prophet for God. Here are 450 prophets of Baal. You call out to your gods and I'll call out to my God; and we will see which God will answer with fire."*

Elijah [YEA!] directed the prophets of Baal to choose a bull and put it on wood, but not to light the fire. They were to call on the name of their gods to light the sacrifice. Elijah [YEA!] would do the same.

The prophets of Baal prepared the bull and put it on the wood. They began to do their ritual worship. From morning until noon there was no fire, no voice, no answer.

Elijah [YEA!] began to poke fun at the priests. He asked them if their god was asleep or on vacation.

The prophets leaped around the sacrifice, cried with loud voices, and cut themselves with knives.

Evening came. No fire, no voice, no answer.

Then it was Elijah's [YEA!] turn.

[Choose three children to help you "build" a pretend altar in front of your back drop.]

Elijah [YEA!] rebuilt an altar to God using twelve stones. Each stone represented one of the twelve tribes of Israel.

[Choose three children to help you "dig" a pretend trench around the altar.]

Elijah [YEA!] then dug a trench all around the altar.

[Choose three children to help you "cut" pretend wood and "place" it on the altar.]

Elijah [YEA!] cut the wood and arranged it on top of the altar. He also placed the sacrificed bull on top of the wood.

[Choose four children to help you "pour water" over the bull, wood, altar, and trench.]

Elijah [YEA!] asked for four water pots to be filled with water and poured over all of the sacrifice, the wood, and the altar. Then he had them do this a second time.

And a third time. Then he made sure the trench was filled with water.

Water was everywhere! The sacrifice was soaked. The wood was soaked. The trench was full of water.

Then Elijah [YEA!] spoke, *"Hear, Lord God of Abraham, Isaac, and Israel. Let it be known today that You are God in Israel. Let these people know that You are the Lord God."*

After Elijah [YEA!] finished praying, FIRE CAME DOWN FROM HEAVEN!

[Be dramatic as you say Elijah's words and have the volunteer toss the "fire" over the backdrop.]

The fire burned up the wet sacrifice, the wet wood, the wet stones, the wet ground, and the water in the trench!!

When the people saw this, they cried out, *"The Lord! He is God!"*

Then Elijah [YEA!] told the people to seize all of the prophets of Baal, and Elijah [YEA!] had them executed.

LIFE APPLICATION

[Ask:]

- *What did Elijah tell the people to choose?* [Either serve God or serve the idol Baal.]
- *The idols the Israelites served were made from wood and metal. What are examples of idols people might have today?* [Possible answers include money, people, good grades, video games, sports, etc.—anything that takes the place of God in our lives.]
- *Can any of those man-made items save you from your sins?* [no]
- *Is there a God who can save you?* [yes]

Yes, God, through the blood sacrifice of Jesus, saves you from your sins. You cannot say that you believe in Jesus and are saved and then allow these other items to be a huge part of your life.

- *Is there anything wrong with playing videos, or ball games, or having a nice car, or clothes?* [no]

No, yet when you focus on those things MORE than God, then you have a problem. What, or WHO, is going to be your God? You cannot serve God and still serve money, games, or school.

- *How can you make sure your focus stays on God first and foremost?* [Allow for answers. They will probably stick with "churchy" answers like go to church and read your Bible. Try to get them to think of everyday things that get in the way, such as choosing to watch TV or read a book before spending time with God in the Bible. Maybe playing sports causes them to have practice or games so frequently that they miss church. Maybe they are too tired to have a family Bible time at home or pray before bed. What do they spend their money on? Etc.]

What is God saying through Elijah and the prophets of Baal? There is only one true God and He wants you to see Him as first in your life. He wants your heart. Choose today whom you will serve . . . and serve wholeheartedly.

COMMENT BOX

THINK: What went well as you taught this lesson? What can you do better?

_____

_____

_____

_____

_____

_____

_____

_____

_____

TIP: Drama can be a powerful tool to teach the Bible to children. Consider having a box of dress-up clothes in your Bible classroom so the children can act out the lessons after you teach. This is a great way to measure how well they listened to you.

9 ELIJAH CHOOSES ELISHA

Mentorship is a vital part of making disciples of Jesus. Use this lesson to teach about the power of God and that people in ministry need other people in ministry.

Scripture Focus: 1 Kings 19:19–21, 2 Kings 2:1–15

Materials:

- Dry ice
- Cooler
- Tongs
- Plastic cup
- Warm water
- Small hand-held fan

Geography: Jordan Valley, halfway between the Dead Sea and the Sea of Kinnereth in the Northern Kingdom of Israel; Gilgal; Bethel; Jericho; Jordan River

Background: Elijah, a prophet to the kings of Israel, had the prophets of Baal killed. He ran away from Queen Jezebel because she wanted him killed. While in hiding, Elijah went to a cave, and God appeared to him as a small voice. God told Elijah to find Elisha to anoint as his replacement.

OBJECT LESSON

■■■■■■■■■■■■■■■■■■

[Place the cup of warm water, fan, and tongs on a table. Have the dry ice nearby in the cooler. Be sure to practice this experiment.]

Whirlwinds, or tornados, are fascinating parts of nature. Scientists are still trying to learn all they can about tornados so they can better warn people when one is created by the weather.

We can create a small whirlwind inside.

[Take the tongs and add 1–2 pieces of dry ice depending upon the size of the cup you are using. Fog should begin to "boil" over. Turn on the fan. Instead of blowing the air toward the fog, flip the fan over so it pulls the fog up through the fan. You should create a small vortex in the fog.]

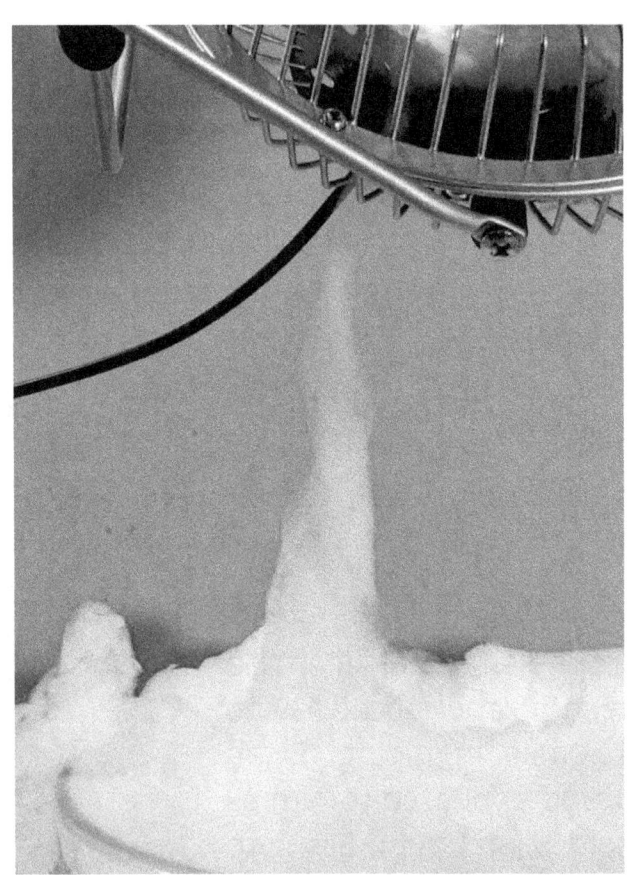

Elijah Chooses Elisha

BIBLE LESSON

A whirlwind plays a part in the Scripture for this lesson. Listen for it.

The prophet Elijah was in a cave where he had a God encounter. There had been a strong wind, an earthquake, and a fire. God had not been in those. Then Elijah heard a soft voice. THAT was the voice of God.

That voice told him that it was time for Elijah to find a student to whom he would pass on his ministry.

[Read 1 Kings 19:19–21. Ask:]

- *Whom did Elijah find?* [Elisha]
- *What was Elisha doing?* [He was plowing the fields; evidently it was a lot of land, because he had twelve pairs of oxen, possibly to rotate through.]
- *How did Elisha know what was going on?* [Elijah threw his mantle (cloak) on him.]

When Elijah put his cloak onto Elisha, it may have been a symbolic expression of handing off his position to Elisha. It is unlikely that the power of God was bound to the garment.

Elisha dropped what he was doing. He told his family goodbye. He may have even had a goodbye party because Elisha sacrificed two oxen. That is a lot of meat!

Then he left with Elijah. He followed Elijah until it was time for Elisha to take over the ministry.

[Read 2 Kings 2:1–15. If you have a map, show the places the men traveled. Ask:]

- *What do we find out in verse 1 that is going to happen?* [The Lord was going to take Elijah up in a whirlwind.]

- *Why do you think Elisha wanted to follow Elijah?* [A possibility is that, considering Elijah is Elisha's father in the faith, Elisha may have hoped that he would receive a blessing from Elijah as fathers gave to their first-born sons.]
- *How did the men get across the river?* [Elijah rolled up his cloak and struck the water. The river split and the men walked over on dry land, just like Moses and the Hebrew people did in Exodus.]
- *In verse 9, what did Elijah finally do?* [He asked Elisha what he wanted, like the giving of a blessing.]
- *For what does Elisha ask?* [a double portion of God's spirit on Elijah to be upon him]
- *Why do you think Elisha asked for that?* [It was a hard request because only God could give this blessing. Elisha was not asking for material blessing, but spiritual blessing so he could take over Elijah's ministry and do well as God's prophet.]
- *What was supposed to happen if God granted Elisha's request?* [If Elisha saw Elijah when he was taken, then the request would be granted. If he did not see him taken, then the request would not be granted.]

[Drop a few more pieces of dry ice into the cup and make a whirlwind again.]

While Elijah and Elisha were walking, a chariot of fire and horses of fire separated the two men. It must have driven between them. Then the whirlwind came and took Elijah to Heaven. The Bible does not say that Elijah rode in the chariot up to Heaven.

Elisha watched all of this happen. He tore his clothes in grief and picked up Elijah's mantle. Then he walked to the Jordan River, split the water again with the cloak, and met a group of young prophets. Those young prophets could tell that the spirit of Elijah was upon Elisha, and they gave him respect.

LIFE APPLICATION

[Ask:]

- *Why do you think Elisha was able to part the Jordan River with the cloak like Elijah had?* [Possibly this was a reminder to Elisha that the same God with the same power who had led Elijah would now lead him.]

During this time in history and culture, horses and chariots were a sign of power in battle. God was showing Elijah and Elisha His power with the horses and chariot of fire. Then, God showed His power again with the splitting of the Jordan River, twice.

- *Can you remember other events of power of which Elijah was a part?* [Allow for answers. Possible answers might be the widow's food multiplying, the widow's son raised, or the fire from heaven that burnt up the altar.]
- *Do you think Elisha had hope about his new ministry with God?* [Yes.]

Elisha knew about these events, and he knew he wanted to demonstrate God's power and wisdom like Elijah.

Elijah had mentored Elisha and prepared him to take over his ministry. It is important for us to learn from people who are older than us. They can tell us about lessons they learned and about God's power in their lives.

God was powerful during the time of Elijah and Elisha. He is just as powerful today. We serve a God who can part the river and take a person to heaven in a whirlwind. This same God raised Jesus from the dead!

We also serve a God who speaks to us in a small voice. We need to be willing to listen to it.

What is God saying through Elijah and Elisha? We are not meant to serve God alone. Elijah needed Elisha just as much as Elisha needed Elijah. Through the power of God, both men served faithfully and communicated God's message of repentance.

COMMENT BOX

THINK: What went well as you taught this lesson? What can you do better?

_____
_____
_____
_____
_____
_____
_____
_____
_____

TIP: Always practice your object lessons before teaching. Some of them can be tricky.

10 ELISHA AND THE WIDOW

The Christian life is one that loves God and loves people. Use this lesson to encourage children to watch for people who need help, especially those who are most vulnerable.

Scripture Focus: 2 Kings 4:1–7

Materials:

- Air-dry modeling clay
- Olive oil
- Wick (pulled from an old candle or purchased in a package; see Resource Page)
- Pencil (for making shape of spout for lamp, and small decorative hole designs, if desired; see picture)
- Matches or lighter to light wick (Please do not leave lamp unattended, or allow children to get too close or touch.)
- Fire extinguisher (just in case)

Preparation:

Make a small clay oil lamp per directions below. If you have the time, resources, and older children, consider having the children make oil lamps from clay as well.

1. Roll a golf ball-sized piece of clay it into a ball.
2. Use a pencil to make a hole in the top of the ball. (Do not let pencil go through bottom.)
3. Pinch around the hole in the top of the clay until you create a round bowl shape. Do not let the edges get too thin.
4. Use a pencil to create a little spout to hold the wick by pinching out a little area, raising it, and then wrapping it around the end of the pencil.
5. Put the wick in spout.
6. Once the basic shape is made, go back and make sure the edges are high enough to hold oil.
7. Then, if desired, use the pencil to make a design on the lamp.
8. Allow the clay to dry before teaching.
9. Go to the Resources Page for a great video showing examples of these lamps and a short explanation devotional.

Elisha and the Widow

Geography: The Northern Kingdom of Israel, 892–832 B.C.

Background: Elisha was a prophet who came after Elijah. He was a disciple of Elijah. He became Elijah's successor, and Elisha was given a double portion of Elijah's spirit—he did twice as many miracles as Elijah. Elisha's name means "God is Salvation." Elisha held the office of "prophet in Israel" from 892–832 B.C., during the reigns of Jehoram, Jehu, Jehoahaz, and Joash of the Northern Kingdom of Israel.

OBJECT LESSON

■ ■ ■ ■ ■ ■ ■ ■ ■ ■ ■ ■ ■ ■ ■ ■ ■ ■ ■ ■

[Ask:]

- *What is light?* [Explain that part of the science of physics studies light, what it is, and what is does. Light consists of electromagnetic waves that travel extremely fast. It is not matter. Light does not need air or water to travel from one place to another. It is similar to the energy that causes ocean waves to move.]
- *Why is light important to us?* [It allows us to see; it causes darkness to go away.]

Elisha and the Widow

BIBLE LESSON

[Ask:]

- *What do you remember about Elisha?* [Review that Elisha was Elijah's follower and servant. When Elijah was taken into heaven, Elisha took over as prophet for Israel. He asked for a double portion of Elijah's spirit, and God graciously granted his request; Elisha did twice as many miracles as Elijah. *If you did not do the lessons in chronological order, then describe Elisha for the children.]

[Read 2 Kings 4:1–7. Ask:]

- *What is a widow?* [A widow is a woman whose husband has died. In Bible times, a widow was often a person who had no protection. Once their husband died, they often had no way of making money for themselves. If their husband left them with no money or with debt, like this widow, they were in real trouble. Losing her home and having no way to feed her children was a real possibility.]

- *Why did the woman go to Elisha for help?* [The woman's husband had been a prophet—a messenger from God, one who served Elisha. She knew that Elisha was the prophet who spoke to kings and commanders on behalf of God's people. She trusted that he would be able to do something for her in her desperate situation.]

- *What did Elisha ask her?* [What do you have in your house?]

- *What did the widow answer to Elisha?* [Nothing, except a flask of olive oil.]

- *What did Elisha tell her to do?* [She was to borrow as many jars as she could from her friends and neighbors. Then she was to go into her house with her sons and start pouring oil into the jars, setting each one aside as it was filled.]

- *What happened when the last jar was filled to the brim with oil?* [The oil stopped flowing. When she told Elisha what happened, he told her to go and sell all the oil. The money made would pay off her debt and allow her and her sons to live.]

- *Why would people have been willing to pay a lot of money for olive oil?* [Allow for answers. Back in Bible times, olive oil was used for more than just cooking. People used it to heal wounds (see Luke 10:34), as a skin soother or cosmetic (see Psalm 104:15), for anointing (see 1 Samuel 16:13), and for light (see Matthew 25:3).]
- *How could people use olive oil for light?* [Allow for answers. It was usually used in small clay lamps, with a bit of cloth or braided string to make a wick, where the lamp was lit. The oil would soak the wick and help it burn steadily and not burn right up, as it would if it were just the cloth or string. Olive oil was a better burning oil than most others they had access to. It was cleaner and burned more brightly.]

[Show the clay lamp. Add some oil and light the wick. Dim the lights and show the video, or if you prefer, sing a hymn or praise song in the light of the lamp.]

BIBLE APPLICATION

[Ask:]

- *How do you think Elisha knew what to do for the widow?* [He was a prophet who heard from God.]
- *Was it Elisha who provided all the oil for the lady and her sons?* [No, it really came from God. He just told Elisha what to do.]

God is full of mercy. Yes, He has rules for us to follow. However, He cares very much for each of you. The rules He gives us in the Bible are there to protect us.

Another way He takes care of people is through those who believe in Him. God showed mercy to the widow through Elisha.

[Ask:]

- *What would have happened if Elisha had ignored the woman?* [Allow for answers. Perhaps she and her sons would have been enslaved to pay off the debt, or they could have died; maybe God would have raised up a different person to show mercy to the woman; Elisha would have missed out on a wonderful miracle of God.]
- *Have you ever stopped to help someone?* [Allow for answers. If the children cannot share an example, share one of yours and discuss the needs met and the blessing of helping.]
- *Have you ever ignored someone who needed help?* [Allow for answers. If the children cannot share an example, share one of yours and discuss why you chose to not help and what you regretted.]

[Point to the lamp.]

Light makes the darkness go away. One way you can act like the light is to help people who need help. Sometimes you do not have to do much. Just smiling at someone can make the darkness go away for that person. Remembering a person's name when no one else does is another way.

[Ask:]

- *Can you think of some other ways you can help others? Be creative!* [Allow for answers.]
- *Who are some people you can help?* [Allow for answers.]

Jesus tells us in the Bible to be the light of the world. The world can have troubles and be a dark place. Elisha is a wonderful example of a light. He knew that God could provide whatever resources the widow needed, and He did.

What is God saying through Elisha? When you choose to be kind, patient, or loving, then you are acting like Elisha. We need to remember that God's resources are limitless and that He cares for those who are most vulnerable.

COMMENT BOX

THINK: What went well as you taught this lesson? What can you do better?

_____
_____
_____
_____
_____
_____
_____
_____
_____
_____

TIP: Spend some time brainstorming ways your class can care for those in need individually, as they see needs each day, and as a class, perhaps as a project or day of service. With younger children, you may have to help them understand what being needy might look like in different situations.

11 ELISHA AND THE SHUNAMMITE WOMAN

■■■■■■■■■■■■■■■■■■■

"You may be the only Jesus someone sees today," is a phrase used in the church. Is it true? Use this object lesson to discuss trusting in God and how Jesus is our Mediator.

Scripture Focus: 2 Kings 4:8–37

Materials:

- Chair
- Pitcher of water with 4 oz. water
- Plastic cup (with white interior)
- ½ tsp. of water gel powder (sodium polyacrylate gel)
- Paper towels (just in case)
- One volunteer

Preparation: Put ½ tsp. of water gel powder in the cup and 4 oz. water in the pitcher before children arrive.

Geography: The Northern Kingdom of Israel in 892–832 B.C.; the town of Shunem, a town between Samaria and Carmel

Background: Elisha traveled around the nation encouraging the people. In this event, the Shunammite woman finds Elisha at Mt. Carmel. This is where his mentor, Elijah, saw fire come down from heaven.

One day Elisha went to Shunem. An important woman lived there. She begged Elisha to stay and eat. So every time Elisha passed by, he stopped there to eat.
—2 Kings 4:8 (ICB)

OBJECT AND BIBLE LESSON

[Place the chair beside you. Have the volunteer come to you. Before they sit down, ask:]

- *Do you trust this chair to hold you up?* [yes]
- *Why?* [If they have sat in chairs that held them up many times, then they will most likely trust a chair to hold them again.]

[Show the cup and the pitcher of water to the children. Tilt it a bit so they can see that nothing is in the cup. Unless they are near to you, they should not be able to see water gel powder in cup. As you pour the water into the cup, say to the volunteer:]

I am going to pour this water over your head, BUT I promise you will not get wet. This is an exercise in trust. I want to see if you trust me.

[Keep holding the cup like it has water in it as the gel absorbs the water. Read 2 Kings 4:8–37, then ask:]

- *Why do you think the woman wanted to put a room in her house for Elisha?* [She recognized that he was a man of God, and she trusted in God, not some of the idols that were so prevalent in that day.]
- *If you were going to build a room on your house for your pastor to stay in when he came by, what would you put in the room?* [Allow for answers.]
- *What did the woman in the story put in the room for Elisha?* [a bed, a table, a chair, and a lamp]
- *Why do you think she put those things in there?* [Allow for answers.]
- *How did Elisha respond?* [He wanted to bless her in some way. He found out that the woman did not have a son and told her that in one year, she would have a son.]
- *Was Elisha correct?* [yes]

This woman and her husband knew that Elisha was a man of God. In those days, many people had turned to idols. They worshipped statues of different things and called them gods. This woman obviously worshipped the one true God and trusted in Him alone. She knew Elisha was a prophet, a messenger of the one true God. She trusted Elisha.

[Ask:]

- *How did the woman show that she trusted God and His messenger, Elisha?* [When her little boy died, she went straight to Elisha, because she knew he would pray to God for her little boy.]
- *When the woman left quickly to go get Elisha, what did she do with her son's body?* [put him on Elisha's bed]
- *Do you think that is what was usually done with a body?* [They probably would have begun preparing the body for burial.]

We are not sure why she put the boy on Elisha's bed, but she trusted that something would be done. Maybe she was expecting and trusting that God, through Elisha His prophet, would wake her little boy up.

Notice how Elisha trusted God, too. He went with the woman as fast as he could, immediately went up to the room, and prayed to God to intercede and to return the little boy to life. God showed him as he prayed what to do to bring the little boy back to life.

[Ask:]

- *Did he come back to life all at once?* [No, first he started getting warm, then finally he sneezed and woke up.]

Sometimes God does miracles all at once; other times He uses a process to do a miracle.

[Consider Mark 7:31-37, Mark 8:22-26, and John 9:1-38 for some examples where Jesus healed using a process, not immediately. Using one or more of these for examples of how God uses a process helps relate this Old Testament story to the gospel. Ask:]

- *How many times did the little boy sneeze?* [He sneezed seven times!]
- *Have you ever sneezed that many times?* [Allow for answers.]

- *What did the woman in this Bible event and Elisha have in common?* [They both believed in the one true God. They both trusted God.]
- *What does it mean to trust?* [Allow for answers.]

In the dictionary it states that "trust" means a firm belief in the reliability, truth, ability, or strength of someone or something.

[Turn to your volunteer and swish the cup around their head.]

(Say the volunteer's name) showed trust in the strength of this chair and its ability to hold him/her up. The Shunammite woman and Elisha both showed trust—belief that God was *reliable*, that He was *able* to heal the little boy, and that He had the *strength* to overcome death. They knew that no man-made god could do this.

We want to see what kind of trust (volunteer name) has in my words. Remember I told him/her that I was going to pour this cup of water over their head, and they would not get wet.

[Ask the volunteer:]

- *Do you believe me when I say you will not get wet?* [Allow for the answer. If they are really fearful and suddenly don't want to volunteer, let them sit down, but let them pick another volunteer.)

[After the volunteer answers, say: *"Here we go!"* Turn the cup upside down without fully inverting it. The gel powder will have absorbed the water and should stay stuck in the bottom of the cup. After a reaction from the volunteer and class, turn the cup quickly right side up. Thank the volunteer for trusting you; then explain the trick.]

BIBLE APPLICATION

■ ■

Elisha, as God's prophet, went to God for the Shunammite woman. The woman trusted Elisha and so she trusted the one true God. Elisha was an example of a mediator, someone who goes between two people.

We have a mediator, too. His name is Jesus. When we decide to follow Jesus, He then goes between us and God. Because of our sin, we have a broken relationship with God the Father. When we look to Jesus, believe that He died for our sins and rose again, and repent, our faith heals that broken relationship. God does not see our sin. Instead, He sees Jesus. Jesus goes between us and God.

Because Jesus is our mediator, we can now go straight to God on our own without having to have a prophet, priest, or pastor go for us. Jesus opened the way to God for us through His death and resurrection. (See Mark 15:38 and Luke 23:45.)

We can be trustworthy like Elisha. When people watch us show honesty and integrity, we can show them Who God is.

[Ask:]

- *What do we trust God for each day?* [Allow for answers. Examples: food, forgiveness, friendship, family, love from God. Remind the children about the Lord's Prayer.]
- *What can we trust God for in our future?* [Allow for answers. Examples: God has a plan for each person; we can spend eternity with Him.]

Some people say, *"You may be the only Jesus someone sees today."* This is true. People cannot see Jesus with their eyes, but they can see what you do for Jesus. When you show love and care, and people trust you, then they might choose to trust in Jesus, too.

What is God saying through Elisha? God uses His people to bring other people to Him. Because of Elisha's kindness and friendship, a woman chose to believe in the power of the one true God.

Elisha and the Shunammite Woman

COMMENT BOX

■ ■ ■ ■ ■ ■ ■ ■ ■ ■ ■ ■ ■ ■ ■ ■ ■ ■ ■ ■

THINK: What went well as you taught this lesson? What can you do better?

_____
_____
_____
_____
_____
_____
_____
_____
_____

TIP: Sometimes it is fun to send the items needed for an object lesson home with your students. This allows the children to reenact the lesson you did and repeat the Bible story at home.

12 OBADIAH AND EDOM

How we treat people matters to God. Use this lesson to teach students how God will judge those who hurt His people, and how to love our enemies.

Scripture Focus: Obadiah 2–4, 10–15, 17–18

Materials:

- Thin cardboard (such as a file folder or cereal box)
- Centimeter ruler
- Pencil
- Scissors
- Bible timeline (if you have one)

The Lord's day of judging
is coming soon to all the nations.
You did evil things to other people.
Those same things will happen to you.
They will come back upon your own head.

— Obadiah 1:15 (ICB)

Preparation: Create a small boomerang. See steps below:

Gather your materials.

Measure 4 cm on one corner of the thick paper.

Measure 4 cm on the other corner.

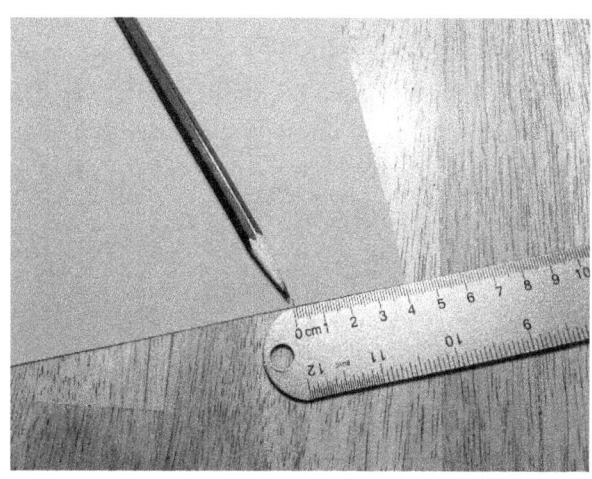

Draw a line 1 cm from the edge at one mark.

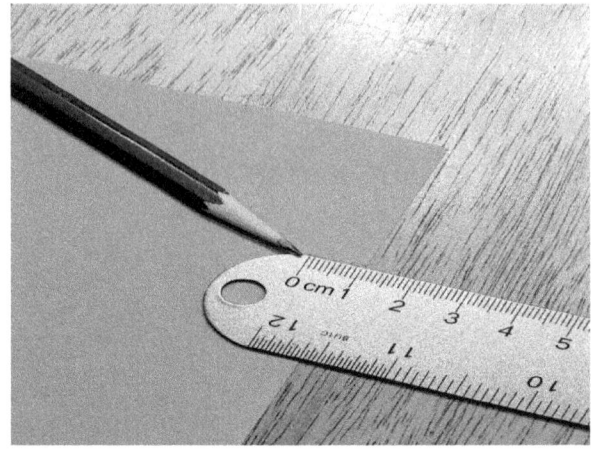

Do the same on the other side.

Create the rectangles that will become the sides of the boomerang.

Cut the boomerang out.

Use the scissors to round the edges and point of the boomerang.

To fly, slightly bend the right side of the boomerang, placing it on two of your fingers. Aim up slightly, being sure the boomerang does not fall off. Use your other hand to flick the right side of the boomerang. It will not be a perfect flight; however, it should turn back toward you and not continue flying straight.

Geography: Edom is the area southeast and southwest of the Dead Sea where the nation of Jordan is today.

Background: Edom was a nation of people who were considered "brothers" of Israel. Isaac had two sons, Esau and Jacob. Isaac's wife had been told by God that the younger son (Jacob) would rule the older son (Esau). Genesis tells us that Jacob stole Esau's blessing and traded soup for his birthright. Because of this, Esau hated his brother. Scripture tells us that Jacob did eventually reunite with Esau in friendship, but as the years went by, the two nations of their descendants were at odds with each other.

When Moses brought the Hebrew people out of Egypt, the king of Edom refused to allow them to travel through his land to reach the Promised Land. Later, Edom opposed King Saul and King David, and Hadad, the Edomite, was an adversary of King Solomon. During the reign of King Jehoram, Edom revolted and Jehoram attacked.

Some scholars believe Obadiah wrote this prophecy to Edom during the reign of Jehoram. Others think it was written as late as when the Babylonians took over.

OBJECT LESSON

[Show the boomerang. Discuss what it is and how it returns to the person who puts it in motion. Flick the small boomerang a few times. Hopefully it will return to you!]

Boomerangs are really neat! If you flick this one just right, it will circle around and come back to you.

Sometimes events in life are like this boomerang. You do something kind for another person and, many times, the person will reciprocate and do something kind back to you.

[Ask:]

- *However, what happens many times when we treat someone badly?* [Discuss some examples; many times, that person will retaliate and be mean back.]

BIBLE LESSON

[If you have a Bible timeline, use it to help you review the patriarchs with the students. Ask:]

- *What do you remember about Esau and Jacob?* [This is a great way to measure Bible knowledge of those whom you are teaching. *If you have not taught the lessons in chronological order, briefly discuss the events of Genesis 25 and following.]

Jacob and Esau had many descendants, and they turned into two nations. Jacob's name was changed to Israel, and that nation came from him. Esau was the father of the nation of Edom. Israel and Edom did not get along with each other because of spiritual and political reasons.

Obadiah was a prophet and was given a message from God to give to Edom.

[Read Obadiah 2–4, 10–15, 17–18. Ask:]

- *What does God say He is going to do to Edom?* [make them small among the nations and greatly despised; covered by shame; cut off]
- *Why?* [Edom was prideful; violent against Israel; watched Israel's distress; rejoiced at their destruction; spoke proudly; cut off Israelites trying to escape and delivered them to the enemy]
- *What do the words "day of the Lord" mean?* [God's judgment, as well as, God's deliverance of those who are faithful to Him]
- *What is God's judgment for Edom?* [What they have done will happen to them; their bad behavior will return upon them; they will become stubble; no survivor will remain.]
- *What does God tell Israel?* [They will be delivered; there will be holiness; they will have their possessions back; they will be like a fire and flame.]
- *How do you think Edom felt about this message?* [Allow for answers. They probably did not like what Obadiah told them.]

- *How do you think Israel felt about this message?* [Allow for answers. Through the ages, Israel consistently watched God take care of His people; this was no different. This message from Obadiah would have given the Israelites hope.]

[Use the timeline to review when the Assyrians and Babylonians took over the lands of Israel.]

When the Babylonians conquered the lands of Israel, they also took the lands of Edom. Many scholars believe that this was the time when Edom was destroyed. The people of Israel were taken into captivity, but not destroyed. Eventually they would come back to their land.

The Edomites treated the Israelites horribly. Israel was God's nation. He was going to always take care of His nation. He will always do what is best for His people.

Remember, Israel was not spared from the Babylonians. They still had a consequence for their sins and disobedience to God; however, they were not wiped out by the enemy. God's discipline was painful and not fun to experience, but its purpose was to cause Israel to be faithful to God's ways again.

It is hard for us to understand the mind of God. He knows everything that has happened throughout history, and everything that will happen in the future. When Jacob and Esau were still inside their mother, God had declared that the younger son would rule the older one. And that is what we see in Scripture.

LIFE APPLICATION

[Show the boomerang.]

This boomerang will come back to the one who throws it. The Edomites were cruel to the Israelites; therefore, their punishment was cruel. God chose to treat them the way they had treated Israel. Their cruelty returned back to them.

Jesus wants us to be different from Edom. Edom was prideful and behaved in mean ways. Jesus tells us that when someone is mean to us, we should not be like the boomerang and return that mean behavior.

Instead, we should try to be kind and patient, showing the fruit of the Holy Spirit. It is a lot easier to be mean back to someone, but God wants us to be like Jesus.

[Ask:]

- *Who was mean to Jesus?* [the Jewish leaders; Roman leaders]
- *Could Jesus have retaliated?* [yes]
- *Why did He not?* [Allow for answers. Jesus understood the mind of God and knew that His death would save people from sin.]

How we treat people matters to God. Through the Holy Spirit we have the power to be loving and kind to those who hurt us. This does not mean that those who do wrong should not have consequences, but it does mean allowing God to be the One who judges and not us.

What is God saying through Obadiah? Edom was destroyed because they were cruel to the Israelites. We can choose to retaliate when others are mean and hurt us, or we can respond with the fruit of the Spirit and allow God to give out the consequences how He chooses.

COMMENT BOX

THINK: What went well as you taught this lesson? What can you do better?

_____
_____
_____
_____
_____
_____
_____
_____
_____
_____

TIP: If you have time, allow the students to create their own boomerangs and have them practice explaining the central truth from this lesson. Encourage them to share this with a friend or adult.

13 JOEL AND THE DAY OF THE LORD

What is the day of the Lord? Has it already happened? Use this object lesson to teach children that God is holy and just, but that He desires to save His people and bless them for eternity.

Scripture Focus: Joel 1:4, 11–16; 2:4–13, 28–32a; Acts 2:16–21

Materials:

- Grasshopper or locust (If possible, catch a live grasshopper to take into class. Place it in a jar with holes in the top so you can let it go afterwards. Use a picture of a locust if you cannot catch one.)
- Watch a video about locust swarms on the Resource Page.

Geography: Jerusalem

Background: Scholars are not sure when the book of Joel was written because there is no reference to a king as in other books of the prophets. One theory has Joel living during the time of Elisha and Obadiah. Another has Joel living later after the return to Jerusalem after the time of captivity. This would make him a contemporary of Ezra and Nehemiah.

"After this, I will give my Spirit freely to all kinds of people. Your sons and daughters will prophesy . . . At that time I will give my Spirit even to servants, both men and women.
— Joel 2:28-29 (ICB)

FUTUREFLYINGSAUCERS.COM

The book of Joel shares content with at least eight other books of Scripture including Isaiah, Nahum, and Malachi. Therefore, either Joel lived before those prophets and was quoted by them, or Joel lived afterwards and quoted the other prophets. Either way, the book of Joel focuses on God confronting evil and His desire to save the world. If Joel was written first, then he is the first prophet to develop the idea of "the day of the Lord" as a description of God's future judgment of the nations.

OBJECT LESSON

■ ■ ■ ■ ■ ■ ■ ■ ■ ■ ■ ■ ■ ■ ■ ■ ■ ■ ■ ■

[Show the grasshopper. Discuss the physical traits of the insect and its actions. Ask:]

- *If we know that one grasshopper can ruin a patch of someone's garden, what do you think thousands of grasshoppers, or locusts, might do?* [Allow for answers. Show the video if you like. Lead the children to understand the destruction locust storms can cause to agriculture. Then, have them think about what that would mean for the people: no food to eat, no food to sell at the market, economic hardship as a nation, etc.]

BIBLE LESSON

Joel wrote about a locust invasion. He could have been describing a swarm of insects that really destroyed the area around him, or, he could have used locusts as a picture of what enemy armies can do.

[Read Joel 1:4, 11–16. Ask:]

- *What types of actions of the locusts are described?* [chewing, swarming, eating, crawling, consuming, etc.]
- *What has been destroyed?* [wheat and barley fields, grape vines, fig trees, pomegranate trees, palm and apple trees]
- *How should the people be responding to the destruction?* [with shame, wailing, withered joy, lamentation, wearing sackcloth, fasting, crying out to the Lord]
- *How does Joel describe this day?* [the day of the Lord]
- *Where did the destruction come from?* [from the Almighty, God]
- *What has been cut off like the food?* [joy and gladness from the house of God; joy of the harvest]

[Show the grasshopper. Say:]

Joel described for us a plague. He called the leaders to mourning and repentance. Remember back to the ten plagues of Egypt during the book of Exodus and the time of Moses. One of the plagues was locusts. Swarms of locusts were seen as a sign of judgment.

Prophets talk about "the day of the Lord," and Bible scholars discuss the meaning of this phrase. Sometimes it refers to when Jesus comes back to Earth. Sometimes it refers to a time when God will pass judgment on people.

In this case, Joel was pleading with his local countrymen to repent and turn back to God. The Lord Almighty will not stand for His people to disobey Him and live in sin. God is holy and just. We will also see that God is merciful.

[Read Joel 2:4–13. Show the grasshopper again. Ask:]

- *What other animal does the head of the grasshopper resemble?* [If you look carefully, the head is extremely similar to a horse's head.]
- *What words are used for the locusts that also sound like an army of horses?* [swift steeds, run, chariots, leap, battle array]
- *What words are used for the locusts that also sound like an army of men?* [climb the walls, march in formation, in ranks, march in column, lunge, weapons, enter like a thief]
- *What words are used for the locusts that sound like a heavenly army?* [earthquakes, heaven trembles, sun and moon grow dark, stars are dim, the Lord commands His army]
- *How is this "day of the Lord" described?* [great and terrible, who can endure it?]
- *How should the people respond?* [They should turn back to God, fast, weep, and mourn. Lead children to understand that all of these words describe an attitude of repentance.]
- *Why should the people return to God?* [because He is gracious, merciful, slow to anger, extremely kind]

Joel described a future day of the Lord. Armies are going to come against Israel, or God's people. This army will bring destruction. God's army will be there, too. God will confront evil and save His people. However, people must repent and turn their whole hearts back to Him. God has a plan. If the people return to Him, then He will refresh the land. He will bless them. There is more to this. And it has to do with us. Joel gave a prophecy that happens in the future.

[Read Joel 2:28–32a, then Acts 2:16–21. Ask:]

- *What is similar in the two passages?* [Peter quotes from the book of Joel on the day of Pentecost.]
- *What was God going to do?* [pour out His Spirit on all flesh]
- *When will this happen?* [in those days]

- *Was this prophecy totally fulfilled on the day of Pentecost?* [No, but part of it was. Peter and the disciples, who were Jews, now had the Holy Spirit, but he did not understand that Gentiles would have the Holy Spirit poured onto them as well. God was still working and teaching.]
- *How are people saved?* [by calling on the name of the Lord]
- *What is the name of the Lord?* [Jesus]

LIFE APPLICATION

■ ■

Through the cross of Jesus, God confronts evil, or sin, for good. Jesus defeated sin by dying and resurrecting from the dead.

[Ask:]

- *What does Joel tell us to do when we realize we have turned from God (sinned)?* [He tells us to repent by mourning and feeling sad over our sin, and to remember that God is gracious and kind.]

There will be another day of the Lord. All of Joel's prophecy has not come about yet. When that day comes, those who choose to follow Jesus have nothing to worry about.

When you choose to believe that Jesus died on the cross, was buried, and rose again, then the Holy Spirit will "pour" over you. He will dwell inside you. It does not hurt. You might not even feel any different. It is comforting to know that the Holy Spirit is with you no matter where you go. He will guide you and help you recognize when you need to repent of something. The Holy Spirit will also encourage you and bring you joy when you do something that honors God.

What is God saying through Joel? The Holy Spirit wants to create fruit in you: love, joy, peace, patience, kindness, goodness, faithfulness, peace, and self-control. If you allow Him to work in you, then when that last "day of the Lord" arrives, you will see Jesus face to face! Glory!!

COMMENT BOX

THINK: What went well as you taught this lesson? What can you do better?

_____
_____
_____
_____
_____
_____
_____
_____
_____
_____

TIP: There is a lot of important scripture in this lesson. If you have a younger group that does not read well, focus on the first two sections.

14 JONAH RUNS AWAY

Many people think the story of Jonah is about a prophet learning to obey God, but is it? Use this object lesson about Jonah to teach that God is sovereign and that He will extend mercy to those who call upon Him.

Scripture Focus: Jonah 1

Materials:

- Whisk

Geography: Nineveh, Tarshish, Joppa

Background: Nineveh was the second largest city of the Assyrian nation, with Babylon being the largest. From Israel, a trip to Nineveh would take about one month over land. Other prophets spoke about the evils of the Assyrians. Nineveh was also known for its temples to many Assyrian gods.

Joppa was about 35 miles south of Samaria on the coast of Israel. This was the opposite direction from Nineveh. Tarshish may have been Tartessus, which was 2,500 miles west in southern Spain and required a boat trip.

Jonah was a prophet to Israel during the time of Jeroboam II, the son of Joash. Shalmaneser IV was king of Assyria. Fifty years after Jonah, Assyria would take the nation of Israel into captivity and scatter the people across many nations.

So the men cried to the Lord, "Lord, please don't let us die because of taking this man's life...Lord, you have caused all this to happen. You wanted it this way."

—Jonah 1:14 (ICB)

OBJECT LESSON

[Ask:]

- *What do you use a whisk for?* [Allow for answers.]

One thing you can do with a whisk is mix ingredients, such as eggs, milk, and sugar. (Use your hand and the whisk to show the motion of stirring.)

Have you ever felt that life seems a little mixed up at times? Like somebody took a big whisk to your life and moved it all around?

Jonah felt a little mixed up.

BIBLE LESSON

[Read Jonah 1. Ask:]

- *Where did God want Jonah to go and what was he to do?* [God wanted Jonah to go to Nineveh and cry out against it. Explain that this meant Jonah was to preach that Nineveh was doomed under God's judgment, and it would be destroyed.]
- *How did Jonah respond?* [He fled to Joppa and got onto a ship going to Tarshish; he wanted to flee from the presence of God.]
- *What did the Lord do?* [caused a strong storm on the sea]
- *How did the sailors feel?* [They were afraid.]
- *What was Jonah doing?* [sleeping in the bottom of the ship]

Nineveh was a large city that belonged to the Assyrian nation. At that time, the Assyrians threatened the Israelites. The Assyrians were bad news.

They were cruel people. They killed men, women, and children. They had temples built to false gods. Jonah knew that Nineveh was the capital of the Assyrians, and God wanted Jonah to tell them that He saw their sin and that they needed to repent.

[Show the whisk.]

Jonah wanted no part in taking any message from God to people whom he hated. Jonah mixed things up by attempting to run away from God.

[Ask:]

- *What did the sailors do to try to save themselves?* [They called on their gods and threw cargo over the side of the ship.]

- *When that did not work, what did they do?* [They cast lots to see whose fault the storm was. Explain that this was a cultural thing to do when decisions needed to be made. Bones or stones would be put into a bag, and one would be drawn out indicating the answer. This is seen in other Scriptures.]
- *Who found Jonah?* [the ship's captain]

This situation is all mixed up. There is a huge problem. The storm was breaking the ship apart. Jonah, the man of God, was sleeping in the bottom away from what was going on. The captain of the ship, who called out to pagan gods, woke up Jonah and urged him to pray to his God. A pagan told a man of God to pray to God.

[Ask:]

- *What did the casting of lots tell the sailors?* [God was punishing Jonah through the storm.]
- *How did Jonah refer to God?* [the One who created the sea and dry land]
- *How did the sailors feel?* [They were terrified.]
- *The sailors knew they had to do something. What did Jonah tell them to do?* [They were to throw Jonah into the sea.]
- *Did they do it?* [They refused at first, because they did not want to kill a man. They attempted to row to shore, but the storm became even stronger.]
- *What did the pagan sailors do?* [They called out to God, begging not to be punished for killing Jonah; they acknowledged His sovereignty and understood that life was in His hands. They did not want to be guilty of murder before God.]
- *What happened after they threw Jonah into the sea?* [The storm stopped; the sailors feared the Lord, offered sacrifices, and vowed to Him. These pagans were praising the Lord!]
- *Was Jonah obedient or disobedient to the Lord?* [disobedient]

Sin has disastrous consequences. God was going to destroy an entire city. Sin hurts people around us. Jonah's disobedience placed the lives of everyone on that ship in danger. Jonah's sin of running totally consumed him. Jonah had turned his back on God.

LIFE APPLICATION

Sin mixes us up. Sin looks good, but it is harmful. Sin can be fun, but it can break relationships.

The entire book of Jonah shows us God's sovereignty. "Sovereignty" is a big word that means *highest power*, or *authority*. God is the main character of the book of Jonah.

God called Jonah.

Jonah ran.

God sent a storm.

Jonah was thrown overboard.

God stopped the storm.

Later in the book, we learn that God sent a fish to swallow Jonah. Then, God had the fish spit, or vomit, Jonah onto land. The people of Nineveh listened to Jonah and did repent. God showed mercy and compassion. Jonah did not.

God was totally in charge of everything that happened, good and bad. He is in charge of everything in your life, too—good and bad.

Many times, people ask the question, *"Why do bad things happen in my life?"* Bad things can happen for a number of reasons. Sometimes we make bad decisions, and then we have bad consequences. Sometimes we make good decisions, but other people make bad decisions, and then we have bad situations. Sometimes we disobey God, and He causes something to happen which we think is bad, so we will turn back to Him.

[Show the whisk.]

We read in the Bible to love people who hurt us. We are told that we are to pray for our enemies. That sounds mixed up. God is going to do what it takes to give people the opportunity to repent.

You know what? The end of the book of Jonah tells us that Jonah continued to have a hard heart towards the Ninevites, even after they had repented. In fact, Jonah became angry with God for being merciful. Jonah was mixed up and needed to repent!

Are you similar to the people of Nineveh? Do you need to repent of sin? Or are you like Jonah, and you need to repent of sin? Either way you look at it, everyone has a need for repentance. It is never too late to repent! We can be like the sailors who recognized who God was, and responded to Him with worship. Go to God and remember that He loves you.

What is God saying through Jonah? God is merciful and kind; He wants to have a relationship with each person. We must repent, recognize who God is, and call on His name to save us from sin.

COMMENT BOX

THINK: What went well as you taught this lesson? What can you do better?

_____
_____
_____
_____
_____
_____
_____
_____
_____
_____

TIP: This is a great Bible lesson to act out. Have volunteers be Jonah, God, the sailors, and the Ninevites. You can drape a blue table cloth over a table and make large eyes to create a fish!

15 AMOS CALLS FOR JUSTICE

■ ■ ■ ■ ■ ■ ■ ■ ■ ■ ■ ■ ■ ■ ■ ■ ■ ■ ■ ■

The Israelites were being accused of bribery, fraud, and hating justice. Use the message of Amos to help your students search their hearts to see if they use authentic worship in their lives.

Scripture Focus: Amos 5:10–15, 20–27

Materials:

- Unused ceramic flower pot
- 1 cup of planting soil
- 1 dead plant
- Box large enough to hold these items
- Beautiful wrapping paper

Geography: Israel, approximately 760–750 B.C.

Background: Amos was a shepherd from the small town of Tekoa, which was about ten miles south of Jerusalem in the Southern Kingdom of Judah. The Hebrew word used for "shepherd" to describe Amos indicates that he might have been a sheep breeder. This means Amos might have owned, or managed, hundreds of sheep and led other shepherds. He is also described as one who grew sycamore fig trees. Therefore, it is quite likely that Amos was a respected man in the community who was a good businessman.

Amos had no training to be a prophet, but God sent him to the Northern Kingdom of Israel during their "golden age," a time of peace and affluence. Assyria was distracted by other nations, which allowed Jeroboam II to increase the territory of Israel. The upper class grew. They built beautiful houses, lived indulgent lifestyles, and used slavery to make people pay debts.

The people were very religious, offering many sacrifices, celebrating festivals, and claiming that God was with them and therefore nothing disastrous could touch them. However, their worship was not authentic, and God was not pleased. Exile was coming, but God always kept a remnant of righteous people.

Preparation: Break the unused flower pot. Place the broken pot, loose soil, and dead plant into the box. Wrap the box in the beautiful paper. Add a bow if you like.

OBJECT LESSON

[Hold out the gift and exclaim how wonderful and beautiful you think the gift is. Describe how excited you are to open the gift.]

I love receiving gifts! When I am given a gift, it tells me that someone thought about me even when I was not physically near to them. It is so special! I feel so loved and appreciated when someone gives me a gift.

[Proceed to open the gift. Have your excited countenance fall as you realize what is in the box. Show the children the broken pieces, the dirt, and the dead plant. Act stunned.]

My heart just fell to the floor. This makes me so sad. I was given a beautiful gift, and it was broken and dead on the inside.

There are times when God feels this way. People offer Him a gift or worship, but instead it is broken and dead.

What God is Saying

BIBLE LESSON

[Read Amos 5:10–13. Ask:]

- *Who is speaking and to whom?* [Lead the children to back up to Amos 5:4. God is speaking to the Israelites.]
- *What do we learn about the Israelites?* [They hated the elders at the gates who maintained justice; abused the poor; took too much grain for taxes; built stone houses; committed mighty sins; afflicted the just; took bribes; and did not allow the poor to have justice.]
- *What do we know about God?* [He knew the sins of the people.]

God knows what is going on the world. He knows the bad things people do. He knows when bad things happen. God knows when poor people are treated badly and when weak people are taken advantage of.

This is what the people of the Northern Kingdom of Israel were doing. Amos was given a strong message for the people of Israel.

Amos was a businessman and farmer who lived in the kingdom of Judah, but God directed him to go to Israel with a message.

[Read Amos 5:20–27. Ask:]

- *How is the day of the Lord described?* [darkness, very dark]
- *What is the Lord not accepting?* [the Israelite's feast days; sacred assemblies; burnt offerings; peace offerings; songs sung; songs played by instruments]
- *What does God want the people to do?* [pour down justice and righteousness like water; in other words, stand for justice and do righteous deeds]

God is disgusted with the worship of the Israelites.

[Show the broken and dead gift.]

This package looked wonderful on the outside, but the inside was broken and dead. What an awful gift to receive!

God felt the same way about the sacrifices and songs of the Israelites. They went through the motions of worship, but in reality, the worship was broken and dead.

God reminded the Israelites that over the years they had had broken worship with Him. In the desert they had worshiped a golden calf. They had also worshiped the sun, moon, and other gods of their own making.

[Ask:]

- *What was to be the punishment for the sins of the Israelites?* [He would send the people into captivity beyond Damascus.]

Damascus was in the direction of Assyria, and the Israelites knew that. God's words would have terrified the people. Captivity meant being taken from their land of promise. The land represented God's presence. In some ways, being in exile and captivity meant being sent away from God's presence.

LIFE APPLICATION

[Read Amos 5:14–15. Ask:]

- *What does God tell the people to seek?* [Seek good, hate evil, love good, and establish justice.]
- *How will God be gracious?* [He will allow a remnant, a small group, of the people to survive.]

God was calling the Israelites to turn away from being mean to the poor and to live righteous lives. He knew that the beautiful songs of worship the Israelites sang were fake because the people lived like they did not care about God or other people He created in His image.

Worshiping God with a beautiful song and then turning around the next day and cheating a person, even selling them into slavery, disgusted God. God knew their worship was not true worship. The worship was fake. The Israelites' gift of worship was broken.

Amos warned them to turn back from their ways, or terrible things would happen. Unfortunately, the people did not listen, and they ended up being overrun by the Assyrian army. The people who managed to survive the attack, the remnant, were carried off to live as slaves in a foreign country.

It is obvious that God wants our whole hearts in worship, not just singing some songs or listening to a sermon.

[Ask:]

- *How can we worship God with our whole hearts?* [Allow for answers. Lead the children to recognize that true worship includes how we treat people, especially people who are poor or different than us.]

Amos had a hard message for the Israelites to hear. This might be a hard lesson for you to hear as well. Think about your actions.

Do not come to church, read your Bible, and sing worship songs and expect God to listen to you if you are mean to people. God wants authentic worship.

[Show the inside of the gift.]

God is the same today as He was in the day of Amos. God is saddened and disgusted by the worship of people when they are not living a righteous life.

[Ask:]

- *Do your actions reflect God's message of seeking good, hating evil, and showing kindness and justice to people?* [Give students time to think; allow for answers.]

What is God saying through Amos? God loves authentic worship. He desires us to seek good, hate evil, and love those who seem unlovable.

COMMENT BOX

THINK: What went well as you taught this lesson? What can you do better?

_____
_____
_____
_____
_____
_____
_____
_____
_____

TIP: This lesson leads to a call of searching one's heart. Consider having the students go into a time of quiet reflection and prayer. Play soft worship music and have the children write a letter to God with their thoughts.

16 HOSEA AND GOMER

Hosea means "salvation," and this object lesson can easily be used in any context where you want to present the gospel.

Scripture Focus: Hosea 1:1–9, 3:1–3

*This Scripture uses words such as "harlot" and "prostitute." If you are teaching younger children, or these words are uncomfortable to use, substitute words such as "an unfaithful wife" or "lived with a man she was not married to."

Materials:

- 2 shoe box-size plastic containers
- Rubber gloves
- Water
- Iodine
- D76 photo developer
- White cloth

Geography: Kingdom of Israel around 739–715 B.C.

Background: Northern Israel, called "Israel," was also known as Ephraim because it was the largest tribe in the kingdom.

It is important to remember the covenant God made with the people at Mt. Sinai. If they obeyed His commands, then He would dwell with them in the land and bless the nation. If the people chose not to obey God, then He warned them about the consequences.

The leaders and people of Israel had broken their part of the covenant. Hosea was given a message which pointed out their sin, the coming judgment, and the final restoration of the people.

[Watch the video on the Resource Page for an example. Be sure to practice and talk through the experiment before you present this to the children. It can be powerful.]

BIBLE LESSON

[Have the two buckets in front of you, but use storytelling for the Bible event first. Read or story tell Hosea 1:1–9.]

Hosea was a prophet who lived in the Northern Kingdom of Israel. The people were far from God. They worshiped idols and did not honor God. God went to Hosea and told him to marry a woman who would not be a faithful wife to him. This sounds really strange. Why would God not want his prophet to have a happy marriage?

God was going to use Hosea's marriage and life as an object lesson for the nation of Israel.

[Ask:]

- *What does the Scripture say as to why God wanted Hosea to take a harlot/Gomer as his wife?* [because Israel had acted like a harlot towards Him]
- *What does it mean to act like a harlot?* [It means to be unfaithful. A spouse who acts like a harlot is one who is not faithful to, who does not honor the marriage commitment of, their marriage partner. So, the people of Israel were not faithful, or loyal, to their commitment to God; they worshiped idols instead.]
- *How many children did Gomer and Hosea have?* [three]

Gomer had three children. The first son was named Jezreel. Names are important in scripture. Jezreel means "God will sow," and in this case, God told Hosea that He would bring about the fall of Israel. A daughter was named Lo-Ruhamah which means "not having received mercy." God wanted Hosea to tell the people that He would no longer have mercy on the nation of Israel. Gomer then had one more son named Lo-Ammi. Lo-Ammi means "not my people."

Wow.

At this point, God was so fed up with the people of Israel that He stated that they would no longer be His people, and He would not be their God.

[Read or story tell Hosea 3:1-3.]

Things look pretty bleak for the people of Israel. Like Gomer, who had been unfaithful to her husband, they were unfaithful towards God. However, God had a plan to bring His people back to Him because He loved them. God told Hosea to find Gomer, pay all her debts, and bring her home. Hosea did this. It is a picture of God bringing a rebellious people back to Himself.

Through the years Israel would rebel against God over and over. God would send His prophets to His people over and over. God is so patient! He loves His people!

LIFE APPLICATION

[Ask:]

- *Are people still rebellious against God?* [Yes! Scripture says that we are born as sinners and enemies of God.]
- *How are you unfaithful to God like Gomer was to Hosea?* [Allow for answers. Help children to think about items or activities that draw them away from God.]
- *What did God do for you that you did not deserve?* [God loved us enough to send Jesus to die on the cross and pay our sin debt. God saves us from sin and eternal separation from Him.]
- *How can you respond to this truth?* [Believe on the Lord Jesus and be saved. Surrender to Him and live a life walking in the ways of God. Love God with all your heart, soul, mind, and strength.]

When we follow Jesus, we can choose to sin against God. We are still sinners while we live on this earth. However, because of the blood of Jesus and the power of the Holy Spirit we can choose to obey God each day. God is patient with us when we fail. Our salvation in Jesus does not go away. Instead, the Holy Spirit will guide and help us to choose righteousness again.

What is God saying through Hosea and Gomer? God takes sin and rebellion seriously. He loves us, but we can be unfaithful to Him. We need to ask the Lord to search our hearts and tell us if we have gone astray so we can repent and get back on the straight and narrow road of walking with Him.

COMMENT BOX

THINK: What went well as you taught this lesson? What can you do better?

_____
_____
_____
_____
_____
_____
_____
_____
_____

TIP: If using this as a gospel presentation, use the resources in the back of this book for how to do this.

17 THE CALLING OF ISAIAH

If God is so powerful and strong, why should we try to do anything for Him? Can He not just do it Himself? Use this lesson to discuss Isaiah's calling by God and God's desire to use imperfect people to display His glory.

Scripture Focus: Isaiah 6:1–8

Materials:

- One piece of unused charcoal, or a piece of coal
- Tongs

Geography: Jerusalem

Background: We know more about Isaiah than about other prophets, but we still do not have much information about him. He probably lived in Jerusalem because he had access to the kings' courts (Kings Uzziah, Jotham, Ahaz, and Hezekiah) and personal access to two kings. Isaiah was married and had two sons. He ministered for at least 58 years. According to tradition, Isaiah was killed by King Manasseh by being sawed in half.

Then I heard the Lord's voice. He said, "Whom can I send? Who will go for us?" So I said, "Here I am. Send me!"
— Isaiah 6:8 (ICB)

The book of Isaiah is first in the prophet's section of the Old Testament. This is because of its size, not because of when it was written.

OBJECT LESSON

[Hold the charcoal/coal with the tongs. Ask:]

- *What this is?* [It is a piece of coal. Explain the difference between coal and charcoal. Coal is a mineral that is formed underground and can be mined, while charcoal is made from wood; both can be burned.]

- *For what is it used?* [Most children will probably say it is used for grilling (charcoal) or heat. However, get them to brainstorm other places they might have seen charcoal, such as in a fish tank filter or humidifier. Fish tanks and humidifiers use charcoal to purify water. Coal is usually burned in factories to create electricity.]

- *When would it be a good time to hold a piece of coal with tongs like these?* [if the coal was hot and needed to be moved]

The Calling of Isaiah

BIBLE LESSON

[Read Isaiah 6:1–8. Ask:]

- *What happened to the king?* [King Uzziah had died.]
- *Who is talking in these verses?* [Isaiah, Seraphim, and God]
- *What does Isaiah see?* [The Lord was sitting on a throne; the Lord was high and lifted up, and the train of the Lord's robe filled the temple. Isaiah also saw Seraphim, which are heavenly beings, (we are not told how many) with two pairs of wings covering their faces and feet, and a third pair of wings used for flying.]
- *What were the Seraphim saying?* ["Holy, holy, holy is the Lord of Hosts; the whole world is full of His glory." (verse 3)]
- *What happened in the temple?* [The posts of the door shook, and the temple filled with smoke.]
- *What do you think Isaiah felt when seeing this?* [Lead them to reread verse 5 and discuss the meanings of these words: woe (great sorrow), undone (not together, not knowing what to do), unclean (not clean, sinful), dwell (live in), hosts (many people).]

Isaiah was watching a vision where he had the blessing of seeing the Lord in His holiness, power, and might. At this point, Isaiah recognized how holy God was. He also recognized how unclean he was. He saw how powerful God was, and how pitiful and small he was. Isaiah realized how majestic and honorable God was, and how worthless and sinful he was.

When we take the time to compare ourselves with God, we should all react the way Isaiah did. He described himself as being *"undone."* Some Bibles use the words *ruined*, *doomed*, or *lost*. Those words help us to understand how Isaiah was feeling.

As the Seraphim were shouting and flying around, as the doors shook, and as the temple filled with smoke, one of the Seraphim used tongs and picked up a heated coal from the altar.

[Hold out the coal using the tongs.]

The Seraphim took the heated coal and touched it to Isaiah's lips.

[Ask:]

- *Why do you think the Seraphim touched the coal to Isaiah's lips?* [Refer back in the verses to Isaiah stating he was a man of unclean lips. God is purity. Humanity is not. The words we speak show our thoughts and feelings which are sinful in many ways. Our thoughts and feelings can become unclean actions. Isaiah knew he was one unclean man living among many people who were also unclean in the sight of a holy God.]
- *The Scripture does not describe the coal as feeling hot and burning Isaiah. What was the purpose for touching the coal to Isaiah?* [Remind the students that coal can be used to purify water. In this case, the hot coal from the altar, when touched to Isaiah's unclean lips, symbolically purified Isaiah and cleaned him of sin. Read verse 7.]
- *What did the Lord ask?* ["Whom shall I send?"]

This chapter of Scripture is sometimes labeled as "Isaiah's Calling." God singled Isaiah out with this vision. The Seraphim cleansed Isaiah with the coal. Then God asked who would serve Him. Isaiah responded that he would go and do what God wanted him to do.

LIFE APPLICATION

■■■■■■■■■■■■■■■■■■■

[Ask:]

- *Have you ever been asked to do something?* [Lead the students to brainstorm events when they have been asked to do something. They might have been asked to take out the trash, or to be a friend to someone. Also discuss how they felt when asked to do certain chores or service. Point out feelings of disrespect, frustration, rebelliousness, excitement, joy, and other attitudes.]
- *How did Isaiah respond when God asked who would go for Him?* [Isaiah immediately told God to send him. This does not mean he was not afraid or nervous. It does show that Isaiah wanted to serve God above all other things.]

After this calling from God, Isaiah declared God's messages to the Israelites. They did not listen to him. In fact, people today would probably say that Isaiah's ministry was a failure. Isaiah obeyed God anyway.

[Hold out the coal again.]

If you follow Jesus, then you have a calling on your life just like Isaiah. Believing in Jesus is like the coal touching your lips. Jesus is the One who makes you clean. Then He tells you to serve Him.

[Ask:]

- *What are some ways you can serve Jesus?* [Possible answers include defending people who are hurt or needy (Proverbs 31:8-9); learning to do right (Isaiah 1:17); giving food to the hungry and clothes to those who need them (Isaiah 58:6-7); loving mercy and being humble (Micah 6:8); seeking first His kingdom (Matthew 6:33); preaching the gospel (Mark 16:15); being patient and loving one another (Ephesians 4:1-6); putting the interests of others before yourself (Philippians 2:1-4); living a holy life (1 Peter 2:9); fixing your thoughts on Jesus (Hebrews 3:1); declaring the praises of God (1 Peter 2:9); using your gifts to serve others (1 Peter 4:10-11).]

You have a calling, and it is important. How God uses you is different than how He uses someone else. You will not be perfect, and you will make mistakes. However, it is through our weaknesses that God displays His majesty and glory to others.

What is God saying through Isaiah? God is mighty, holy, and powerful, and He desires to use people to bring about His glory. God wants to use you to show His glory to those around you.

The Calling of Isaiah

COMMENT BOX

THINK: What went well as you taught this lesson? What can you do better?

_____
_____
_____
_____
_____
_____
_____
_____
_____

TIP: This would be a great lesson to teach in conjunction with a service project. Discuss how God has gifted each person in the group and how they can serve others in this particular situation.

18 ISAIAH AND THE COMING MESSIAH

▎▎▎▎▎▎▎▎▎▎▎▎▎▎▎▎▎▎▎▎

There are many announcements about the birth of Jesus in the Bible, but this one in Isaiah tells us so much about the character of God. Use this lesson to show that a prophecy was fulfilled and that God does what He says He will do.

Scripture Focus: Isaiah 9:1–7 (focus on verses 6–7)

Materials:

- A birth certificate or baby announcement (with a baby's footprint on it, if possible)
- Parchment or craft paper, cut in 4 in. x 6 in. (10.2 cm x 15.2 cm) rectangles (enough for one per child)
- Washable stamp pad (black)
- Hand wipes
- Hole punch
- Ribbon (enough to make a loop to hang on tree)
- Isaiah 9:6 verse printed and cut out to fit onto the paper rectangle
- Glue stick

*Activity is optional.

A child will be born to us. God will give a son to us. He will be responsible for leading the people. His name will be Wonderful Counselor, Powerful God, Father Who Lives Forever, Prince of Peace.
— Isaiah 9:6 (ICB)

Geography: Judah in approximately 740–687 B.C.

Isaiah and the Coming Messiah

Background: Isaiah was a prophet and advisor to kings during the reigns of Uzziah, Jotham, Ahaz, and Hezekiah. Around 740 B.C., Isaiah had visions of calling while in the temple of Jerusalem. God warned him that his ministry would be disappointing, but that forgiveness and God's promises would come to pass. Isaiah knew what was going on politically and economically in Israel and in the surrounding nations. He encouraged the kings of Judah to stay neutral as much as possible.

In his writing, Isaiah focused on showing that God was the ultimate King. Israel was a sinful nation filled with sinful people. Isaiah clung to the hope of forgiveness and the future Messiah.

OBJECT AND BIBLE LESSON

■■■■■■■■■■■■■■■■■■■■

[Show the birth announcement or certificate. Ask:]

- *What is this?* [Explain what it is.]
- *What information does a birth announcement give?* [name of the baby, the date it was born, and maybe the time and weight]
- *What information do you know about your birth?* [Have them give similar details as the announcement. If they do not know, give details about your birth.]

The Bible passage we read today was also a birth announcement. It tells us about the birth of the Messiah.

[Read Isaiah 9:1–7 and have the children let you know when they hear details about the birth of the Messiah: where He would live (Galilee), that the child born would be a boy, that He would be a descendant of David and would be King, His names, etc.]

We do not have a cute birth announcement, or certificate, with baby Jesus' footprints on them. But we do have this prophecy from Isaiah over 700 years before Jesus was born.

God's people were the Israelites. They knew the Rescuer and the Savior was coming. They knew He would rescue them, and He would be King. They thought He was rescuing them from the countries that were taking over and oppressing them. They thought that He would become King of Israel after He conquered those others who had taken over Israel.

[Ask:]

- *In verse 1, which place name sounds most familiar to you?* [Jordan and Galilee might sound familiar; Jesus grew up in the area of Galilee and was baptized in the Jordan River.]
- *What is in darkness?* [the people, those who dwelt in the land]
- *What did they see?* [a great light]

When the Hebrews settled in the land of Israel, they were separated into twelve tribes. Two of them were Zebulun and Naphtali. Their sections of land were near the Sea of Galilee.

[Read Matthew 4:15–16.]

- *What did you hear in Matthew's verses?* [Explain that Matthew focused on showing how prophecy was fulfilled in Jesus.]

[Read Isaiah 9:3–5 again. Ask:]

- *Who do you think the YOU is in these verses?* [God]
- *What did God do, or what is He going to do?* [multiplied the nation, increased Israel's joy, and broke the yoke of Israel's burden]

God was going to save His people from oppression. What they did not know was that Jesus had a much bigger plan than saving Judah from the nations around it! He came to free them from sin. God would eventually save them from their earthly oppressors, but He would send Jesus to save ALL people from the one who was at the root of all the oppression—Satan. Jesus came to save us by conquering sin, death, and Satan. He did all of that! They thought He came to be King, but Jesus came to show He's already King—the King of heaven and earth.

Bible Activity (Optional):

1. Give each child a parchment paper piece, a printed verse, a glue stick, and a piece of ribbon.

2. Have each child make a fist with their left hand. One at a time, place the left side of the fist into the black stamp pad.

3. Immediately press their fist carefully onto the middle of the parchment paper. This makes the "foot" part of the baby announcement. (See pictures.)

4. Have each child press his left or right index finger into the stamp pad and put five little "toes" on top of the foot.

5. Have them wipe off their hands with the hand wipes, then glue their verse onto the bottom of the paper.

6. Punch a hole at the top of the paper and thread a piece of ribbon through it, tying at the top.

7. You can leave these as they are, or roll them up like a scroll. (This ornament works beautifully with the first Sunday of Advent when the candle of Hope, or Prophecy, is lit.)

LIFE APPLICATION

[Hold up one of the ornaments. *If you did not do the ornaments, see the life application section below.]

Now you have a birth announcement for Jesus! You can share the good and exciting news that Jesus was born to save us from our sin.

[Help the children to think of a friend who needs to hear about Jesus. Challenge them to give their ornament away to that person.]

[*If you did not do the ornaments, hold up the birth certificate.]

The birth of Jesus was announced by Isaiah and other prophets years before He was born. He was announced by name.

[Ask:]

- *Can you think of another announcement about Jesus being born? To whom was the announcement made?* [Possible answers include the angels' announcements to Zacharias, Mary, the shepherds, and the star appearing to the wise men.]

We can be certain that if God says He is going to do something, then He will do it. Isaiah 9:7 tells us that the zeal of the Lord would bring about this child that was to be born. God did it. Jesus was born.

Every day we can remember that we have a Wonderful Counselor whenever we need advice or someone to talk to. We have a Mighty God who can do all things. Jesus is the Everlasting Father. This tells us that He protects His people. And the Prince of Peace will help us when crazy and hard events happen in our lives.

This is amazing and worth telling others. Jesus is worthy of our time and effort.

What is God saying through Isaiah? A Baby was going to be born and He would be more powerful than any government. He would be a King at His birth. God did what He said He would do!

COMMENT BOX

THINK: What went well as you taught this lesson? What can you do better?

_____
_____
_____
_____
_____
_____
_____
_____
_____

TIP: There are promises of God to Jesus' followers in the New Testament. Discuss these with your students. (James 1:5, 1 Corinthians 10:13, John 10:28–29, Hebrews 13:5, Philippians 1:6, Luke 12:40)

19 MICAH'S PROPHECY: BIG NEWS ABOUT A TINY PLACE

The fulfillment of the birth of Jesus, the Messiah, is important because it proves the faithfulness of God. Use this lesson on Micah's prophecy to help build confidence in the promises of God.

Scripture Focus: Micah 5:2–5

Materials:

- Small water bottle (10 oz.) half-filled with water
- 2 tsp. white sugar
- 1 packet of active yeast
- Small funnel
- 1 balloon (The balloon needs to be a thin, low-quality balloon. The experiment does not work as well with a thicker balloon.)

Geography: Israel and Judah in the latter half of the 8th century B.C.

Background: Micah prophesied during the reigns of Jotham, Ahaz, and Hezekiah. The Israelites were insulting God with idol worship *"in every corner"* (2 Chronicles 28:24). Micah prophesied judgment through the armies of the Assyrians on Israel and Judah for their idolatry, but he also prophesied hope in the form of a Shepherd King to come, who would not only restore their peace, but be their peace.

But you, Bethlehem Ephrathah, are one of the smallest towns in Judah. But from you will come one who will rule Israel for me. He comes from very old times, from days long ago.

— Micah 5:2 (ICB)

OBJECT LESSON

[Show the packet of yeast. Ask if anyone knows what it is, or what it does. Open the yeast, pour some in the palm of your hand, and show how tiny the yeast particles are. Explain that these are budding, single-cell fungi that are used in baking to cause breads and cakes to rise.]

It is amazing how small yeast can cause a ball of dough to rise and make a larger loaf of bread!

[Ask:]

- *Can you think of something else that starts out very small and turns into something much bigger and more wonderful?* [Allow for answers, such as seed/flower, match/fire, threads/clothing, for example.]

Today we are going to let the tiny yeast do something different than causing bread to rise. We are going to let them partly blow up a balloon!

[Funnel two teaspoons of sugar into the half-filled water bottle. Swirl it around to mix. Open the yeast packet and funnel it into the bottle. Swirl it around in the bottle to mix. Stretch the balloon opening first, then carefully stretch it and place it over the mouth of the bottle. Set the bottle and balloon aside, or put a box over it so the children cannot see it.]

This experiment does not happen all at once—we have to wait for it.

[Ask:]

- *Can you think of something for which you had to wait?* [Allow for answers.]
- *Are you waiting for something right now?* [Allow for answers.]

This experiment reminds us of a time of waiting for God's people, both the Israelites in the time of the prophets, and God's people now—us!

Micah's Prophecy: Big News About a Tiny Place

BIBLE LESSON

The prophet Micah prophesied about 700 years before Jesus was born. Micah was a prophet during the reign of three different kings—Jotham, Ahaz, and Hezekiah. He lived in Judah, the southern part of Israel, but his prophecies were for northern Israel and southern Judah.

The Israelites, God's people, had turned away from God and were worshipping idols, copying the people of the countries all around them. Micah kept telling the people that a terrible judgment was going to come on Israel and Judah if they did not turn away from their idolatry. He prophesied that the Assyrian armies were going to sweep through their lands and destroy everything, kill people, and take the rest away as captive slaves. Micah told the people that God had a rescue plan.

[Read Micah 5:2–5. Ask:]

- *Who is Micah talking about?* [Jesus]

Micah was prophesying several things about Jesus here. Remember, prophesying means that Micah was getting a message from God to deliver to the people. He was not just predicting out of his own head, or making wishes.

God's prophecies will 100% come true. God is in charge and can see all the future and all the past.

Look at the first prophecy: *"But you, Bethlehem Ephrathah . . ."* There was more than one Bethlehem. God gave Micah the name of this exact village, Bethlehem Ephrathah. This particular Bethlehem was just south of Jerusalem, while the second Bethlehem was in the northern portion of Israel near Galilee.

Look at the next part of the prophecy: *". . . who are too little to be among the clans of Judah . . ."* Bethlehem Ephrathah, or Bethlehem Judah, was a small village, unimportant in every way, EXCEPT that God planned for His Rescuer to come from there. Just like the yeast are tiny and cause the dough to become larger, this little town was going to have something BIG happen in it.

[Ask:]

- *Where was Jesus born?* [Bethlehem, just a few miles away from Jerusalem in the southern part of Israel]

It was this exact Bethlehem. Micah had prophesied that God's Messiah, the Rescuer, would be born in this particular tiny Bethlehem over 700 years before Jesus was born! Wow! That would be way more incredible than if George Washington, who lived only 250 years ago, predicted that **(say the name of a child in the room)** would be born in **(say the name of a small town)**!

God gave Micah the message, so he knew it had to be true. He told God's people that they could count on God's Rescuer being born in Bethlehem, but they did not know when. Remember we said we would have to wait to see what would happen with our experiment? God's people had to wait . . . and wait . . . and wait. Finally, 700 years after Micah's prophecy, Jesus was born in Bethlehem, just like God said He would be. We can always count on God's promises.

Let's see how our experiment is going.

[Take out the water bottle/yeast/balloon and look at the difference since you first put the yeast in. You can keep it in sight through the remainder of the session.]

LIFE APPLICATION

[Read Micah 5:4–5. Ask:]

- *In Jesus' day, was He great, or famous, "to the ends of the earth"?* [no]

Jesus' followers started off with a small handful of disciples, but, like the tiny yeast grew and grew, believers in Jesus have grown in number for over 2,000 years. Jesus' followers are all over the globe, in many countries, speaking many languages.

Micah says, "*He will be great to the ends of the earth.*" So now, just like God's people had to wait for God's Rescuer to come the first time, we have to wait for Him to come back again. Then everyone, in every nation, tribe, and language will know of the greatness of Jesus!

[Ask:]

- *How can we help grow God's kingdom—the followers of Jesus?* [Allow for answers.]

We help grow the kingdom by telling the people around us about Jesus. Then they tell others, and they tell others, and so on.

[Ask:]

- *How does knowing the accuracy of the Bethlehem prophecy help us with all the other many prophecies about Jesus?* [We can be confident that the scriptures are trustworthy.]

What God is Saying

What was God saying through Micah? We can trust God to do what He says He will do. We might have to wait, like we waited on our experiment. We might have to wait like the Israelites waited on the Messiah to be born. Yet, we can be sure that God will keep ALL His promises.

Micah's Prophecy: Big News About a Tiny Place

COMMENT BOX

■ ■

THINK: What went well as you taught this lesson? What can you do better?

_____
_____
_____
_____
_____
_____
_____
_____
_____
_____

TIP: One day people of all nations will be proclaiming the name of Jesus. Show the video The World Blessing 2023 on the Resource Page and have the students look at the different flags, skin colors, faces that are blurred, languages, and abilities. All nations will be represented in Heaven with Jesus.

20 NAHUM, NINEVEH, AND JUDAH

Scripture tells us that God will extend vengeance on His enemies. Who are God's enemies? Use this lesson to teach that God is in control of everything, even those who treat other people in terrible ways.

Scripture Focus: Nahum 1:1–8; Psalm 146:5–10

Materials:

- Picture of someone who is precious to you (your own children, grandchildren, spouse, or close friend)

Geography: Nineveh between 663–612 B.C.

Background: Nineveh was an old city in Assyria. It had been built by Nimrod (Genesis 10:8–12). Over the centuries, Assyria attacked many nations all around it, including Israel. King Shalmaneser III, a king of Assyria, wrote that he had fought Ahab the Israelite and had taken tribute from Jehu, son of Omri. This writing is on the Black Obelisk of Shalmaneser. Neither of these events are mentioned in the Bible. (See a picture of the obelisk on the Resource Page.)

One hundred years before Nahum, Jonah preached to the Ninevites, and they repented. However, over time, the Ninevites

Nahum, Nineveh, and Judah

went back to their old ways. Nahum was a prophet in Judah, probably during the reign of Manasseh while under the yoke of Assyria. The Ninevites were the enemy, but Nahum prophesied that Assyria would fall and be destroyed. While this would be terrible for Nineveh and Assyria, this destruction would bring comfort to those in Judah.

OBJECT LESSON

[Show the picture and explain who it is and why the person is so precious to you.]

This is (person's name), and I love this person dearly. I care for this person. I spend time with this person. I give gifts to this person. If something were to threaten this person, or cause them to be in danger, I would do everything in my power to protect this person.

[Ask:]

- *Do you have a person you love dearly?* [Allow for answers.]

I would do anything in my power to protect this person. I bet you would protect your person, too. If someone tried to hurt (person's name), I would become angry and try to get that person away from harm.

BIBLE LESSON

God does the same thing!

[Read Nahum 1:1–8. Ask:]

- *To whom was Nahum speaking?* [Nineveh of Assyria]
- *Who else had had a message for Nineveh?* [Jonah, about 100 years earlier]
- *What words are used to describe God?* [jealous, avenger, furious, vengeance, wrath, slow to anger, great in power, He has His way, rebukes the sea, fierce, good, knows who trusts Him]
- *What feelings do you have when you hear those words said about God?* [Allow for answers.]

There is a mixture of words used about God in these Scriptures. Some of the words make God sound angry and mean. We must remember that God is all powerful, but He is also good, faithful, and merciful to those who trust in Him.

Nahum told Nineveh this message. Nineveh was one of the largest cities of Assyria, which was the main enemy of the kingdom of Judah at this time. The king of Assyria forced the king of Judah to pay tribute to him. This meant the king of Judah had to pay money to Assyria so they would not attack them.

Assyria was a ruthless nation. They killed and took over towns. The people of Judah were tormented by the Assyrians even though the king paid tribute. The people were surrounded by Assyrians as they took more and more land.

Judah was a nation that belonged to God. Remember that God gave the Hebrew people this land. He gave them the ability to have a great nation. Now this small nation was being bullied and hurt by a larger nation.

God became angry. He became jealous. "Jealous" can have two different meanings. We can be jealous of someone when we want what someone has. God is not jealous of people. He does not need anything from us.

The definition of jealous that describes God means to fiercely desire the best for someone. Instead of being jealous OF someone, God is jealous FOR people. He wants to see good things happen to those who belong to Him. He wants to protect His people from harm. God is against anything that can hurt us, especially sin.

God was jealous for the kingdom of Judah. God would do anything to bring the people of Judah back to Him.

With us thinking this way, let us look back through these verses and find words that show us God was jealous for Judah.

[Allow for answers. The Lord takes vengeance on adversaries; darkness will pursue His enemies. Ask:]

- *What does God think about Nineveh?* [He sees them as the enemy.]
- *What is a stronghold?* [A stronghold used to be the main place in the city where people could run when an enemy attacked, such as the inside of a castle.]
- *What was God saying about Himself to Judah?* [He is good; He is the place to run to when there is trouble; He knows those who trust in Him.]
- *What does God control?* [He controls everything: the whirlwind, the storm, clouds, the sea, mountains, the world.]
- *How does it make you feel to know that God has everything in the world under His control?* [It should bring comfort; like a parent is in control of the home, God controls everything in the universe.]

History teaches us that the Babylonians conquered Assyria and destroyed Nineveh, just as Nahum described. In fact, Nineveh is still in ruins. God attacked the enemy, not when Judah wanted Him to, but when God knew it was the right time.

Nahum's prophecy was one of destruction for Assyria, but one of comfort for Judah reminding them that God was in control.

LIFE APPLICATION

[Show the picture of your loved one again. Ask:]

- *Who is the person who loves you?* [Examples might be parents, grandparents, a good friend, aunts or uncles. Be aware of children from broken homes, etc.]
- *How do you know that God loves you?* [Allow for answers; help the children think through ideas such as blessings He has given, protection, maybe something happened, or did not happen, that did not seem good at the time, but now can be seen as a good thing; the greatest way we know that God loves us is that He sent Jesus do die on the cross for us while we were still in our sin.]

[Read Psalm 146: 5–10. Ask:]

- *What do these verses tell us about people?* [Those who turn to God are blessed; their hope is in Him]
- *What do we learn about God?* [He made the heavens, the earth, and the sea and everything in them; makes justice happen for the oppressed; gives food to the hungry; gives freedom to prisoners; opens the eyes of the blind; raises those who are bowed down; loves the righteous; watches over strangers; takes care of the orphans and widows; He will reign forever]
- *Who else does this sound like?* [Jesus]
- *What happens to the wicked?* [God turns their ways upside down]

The ways of the Assyrians were definitely turned upside down! Again, we read verses that remind us that God is in control of everything.

You need to remember that God is in control of everything, especially when seemingly bad things happen around you or to you. Scripture tells you to turn to God who is like a strong castle that protects us.

There are other things listed in this Psalm that tell you what God is doing around you. God is always at work. He is watching over people, righting wrongs, taking care of widows and orphans, giving food to the hungry, and so much more. This sounds a lot like Jesus!

When we realize that we have sinned against God and turn to Jesus for salvation, God brings us back into fellowship with Him and comforts us with grace and mercy. In response to this, we then live a life that reflects Jesus and show that same grace and mercy to those around us. If you want to live like Jesus, then you should do similar activities that He did.

Jesus can do anything by Himself, but most of the time He uses His Church to do His work in the world. You can allow Jesus to use you to bring comfort to others like Nahum brought comfort to the nation of Judah.

What is God saying through Nahum? God is trustworthy and in control of everything. He is jealous for you. God wants us to turn to Him for comfort and then turn around and show comfort to others.

COMMENT BOX

THINK: What went well as you taught this lesson? What can you do better?

_____
_____
_____
_____
_____
_____
_____
_____
_____

TIP: Brainstorm with the children ways to help, or support, local foster care families, or nursing homes. Then do something to help.

21 ZEPHANIAH AND THE RESTORATION OF JUDAH

The people of Judah were choosing to worship idols instead of God. Because of this, Zephaniah warned the people of imminent doom and punishment. Use this lesson to teach how God remembers His remnant in the midst of His anger.

Scripture Focus: Zephaniah 1:2–3, 6; 2:3; 3:13–20

Materials:

- A baby doll, or real baby
- Lullabies (See the Resource Page for two example videos.)

Geography: Judah in approximately 640–609 B.C.

Background: The prophet Zephaniah lived and prophesied in a time of real trouble. King Josiah had brought about reform in Judah. He got rid of idols and started reading God's word to His people for the first time in many, many years. But the hearts of the people were far from God. They loved to worship idols and do the same things as the countries around them, even though God had warned them again and again that

The Lord your God is with you.
The mighty One will save you.
The Lord will be happy with you.
You will rest in his love.
He will sing and
be joyful about you."
— Zephaniah 3:17 (ICB)

terrible things would happen if they turned away from worshipping the one true God.

At the beginning of the book of Zephaniah, the prophet, took the time to make sure the reader understood that the words he was writing came from God. Then Zephaniah described his family background. One of the people mentioned was Hezekiah, which some scholars believe was the same person as the king, which means Zephaniah could have been royalty.

Zephaniah wrote about two themes. One is the strong call for repentance because of the sin of the people. The second is the comforting truth that God does not forget His mercies even when bringing judgment.

OBJECT LESSON

[Show the doll or real baby. Ask:]

- *Do any of you have a baby at your house?* [Allow for answers.]
- *What are some things we know about babies?* [Lead the children to think about what babies do, what their families have to do, and what they like most about babies.]

BIBLE LESSON

[Read Zephaniah 1:2–3, 6. Ask:]

- *What do you feel when we read these verses?* [These verses can seem scary; God might be talking about reversing His creation because the order in which He will consume is: man – beast – birds – fish, which is the opposite order in which He created the world.]
- *Verse 3 tells us that God will cut off man. What type of man?* [Read verse 6 again; God will cut off those who have turned their backs on Him, who do not seek Him, nor talk to Him.]
- *How do you think the people of Judah felt when they heard these words from God?* [Considering many of the people of Judah were far from God, they may not have listened to Zephaniah; however, there is always a remnant who will listen.]

Sometimes the Bible has some scary verses. Many of these warnings were to specific groups of people. However, we can learn from God's interaction with His people. It is important for us to remember that God is holy, which means He is set apart from people. He is set apart from sin. God is perfect.

[Ask:]

- *If someone chooses to do something that is against government law, what usually happens?* [Usually, the police arrest them and they go before a judge for a punishment; sometimes the punishment is to go to jail and be separated from their family and friends for a certain amount of time.]

God is a perfect judge and Zephaniah was warning the Israelites that God was going to punish them.

[Read Zephaniah 2:3. Ask:]

- *What does Zephaniah tell the people to do?* [Seek the Lord; uphold God's justice; seek righteousness; seek humility.]

- *What might happen if the people do these things?* [They might be hidden from the Lord's anger.]

Zephaniah wanted the people of Judah to understand that if they chose to seek the Lord and follow Him, then they would be sheltered when God's punishment came. This meant that a remnant, or a small group, of people from Judah would live through God's punishment of the nation of Judah.

Eventually the Babylonians attacked the kingdom of Judah, and Zephaniah's prophecy was fulfilled. Many people of Judah were killed. However, the Babylonians exiled, or took out, a group of people from Judah to live in Babylon.

[See if the children can think of a Bible story of people from Judah in Babylon: Daniel, Shadrach, Meshach, and Abednego. Read Zephaniah 3:14–17. Ask:]

- *How do these verses make you feel?* [Allow for answers.]
- *How do you think the remnant of Judah felt about these words?* [Those who were in exile held on to these words with the hope that God would allow them to go back to Jerusalem one day.]
- *What will God do for His people?* [take away their sin; cast away their enemy; no more disaster; save]
- *What will God do over His people?* [rejoice with gladness; quiet with love; rejoice with singing]
- *Who is the Mighty One who will save?* [Jesus]

The people of Judah thought this prophecy was about them returning to their land and God setting them back up with a king. Instead, God was doing a larger work. He was planning to send Jesus, who would save people from their sin, cast away the enemy of death, and allow us access to heaven where there will be no more disaster.

Those who choose to follow Jesus are rejoiced over! God quiets us with His love and rejoices over us with singing.

LIFE APPLICATION

We talked about what babies do. Some things are super cute, and others not so much. One thing all babies do is cry. They cry at different times, sometimes when they're hungry, or sleepy, or scared.

Zephaniah says that God would quiet His people with His love.

[Ask:]

- *How does a caregiver quiet a baby?* [Allow for answers.]
- *Often, caregivers will hold and calm their babies by singing over them. Has anyone ever heard of a lullaby?* [It's a song sung especially to calm the baby and help it rest.]

God's true Word tells us, "*He will quiet you with His love, He will rejoice over you with singing.*" God actually sings. He created music. He sings about His love for us, calms us, and quiets us. He does this in the middle of our stress, anxiety, and troubles. He is our Father, and He sings over His children.

God hates sin. It makes Him angry. Because He loves us so much, He sent Jesus to live on the Earth, die on the cross, and rise again. When Jesus died on the cross, He settled our sin problem. This means your sin is forgiven and Jesus took care of the judgement of sin. When you believe in Jesus and follow Him, you get to be a part of the new remnant! There is no judgement and you are a part of the family of God.

Next time you are upset about something, seek God, who is your Heavenly Father; try to imagine God holding you, calming you, and singing over you!

What is God saying through Zephaniah? God is just and holy. He will punish those who choose to turn away from Him. However, God remembers those who seek Him, and He will rejoice and sing over them.

COMMENT BOX

■■■■■■■■■■■■■■■■■■■■

THINK: What went well as you taught this lesson? What can you do better?

_____

_____

_____

_____

_____

_____

_____

_____

_____

TIP: Give kids the opportunity to imagine what it is like when God *"quiets us with His love,"* and *"rejoices over us with singing."* Allow them to listen to lullabies or reflective music and write or draw their response to that idea.

22 JEREMIAH AND JEHOIAKIM

The prophet Jeremiah had a strong word from God for the King of Judah. Would he listen? Use an optical illusion to teach children to not just listen to the word of God, but to do what it says.

Scripture Focus: Jeremiah 36; James 1:22

Materials:

- 3 pieces of copy paper
- 1 piece of construction paper
- Scissors
- Glue

Geography: Kingdom of Judah; 627 B.C.

Background: The nation of Israel had been divided after the reign of Solomon. Northern Israel had no good kings, while southern Judah had a few good kings.

Jeremiah's ministry spanned the last fifty years of Judah's existence. Judah's last good king was Josiah. In 622 B.C., the Law had been found, and spiritual renewal had spread across the kingdom. After Josiah was killed in battle (609 B.C.), Judah returned to their sinful ways.

Jeremiah, get a scroll. Write on it all the words I have spoken to you about Israel and Judah and all the nations. Write everything I have spoken to you since Josiah was king until now.
— Jeremiah 36:2 (ICB)

Preparation: You will be using an optical illusion for the object lesson, so be sure to have it ready before you have children in the room with you. See the images for directions.

Step 1: Cut a sheet of copy paper with three slits as shown. (Don't actually make the dashes on the paper. Keep it white.)

Step 2: Hold the short ends of the paper and twist 180 degrees.

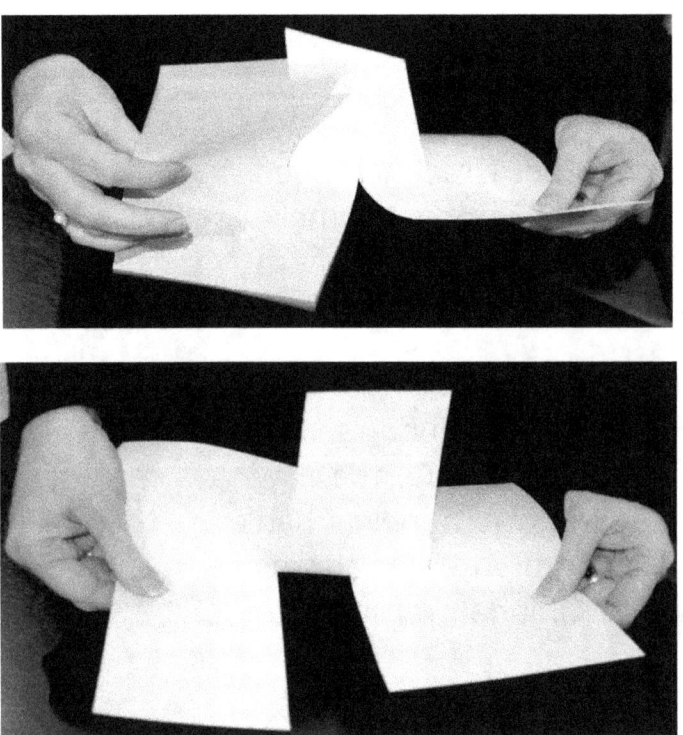

Step 3: Glue it onto a sheet of construction paper.

OBJECT LESSON

[Ask for a volunteer to help you. Show your illusion and ask:]

- *I am going to give you a sheet of paper. Do you think you can create this illusion?* [Allow for answers from the volunteer.]

[Give the volunteer time to look at yours and try to recreate it using the scissors. If they seem stuck say, "You can ask anyone in the room for help." The volunteer will probably ask for help from a friend or another child. After another few moments ask:]

- *Why did you ask (person's name) to help you?* [Allow for answer.]
- *Who is the person in this room who knows how this illusion was created?* [You are.]
- *Why did you not ask me for directions?* [Allow for answer and some laughs; if, by chance, the volunteer DID ask you how to do it, then commend them on going to the best source of information.]

I am going to show you how to do this illusion at the end of our lesson because I want you to be able to share this with others. For now, let us discuss the people of Judah who did not listen when God gave them instructions.

BIBLE LESSON

[Depending upon the age of the children being taught, you might want to read the entire chapter of Jeremiah 36. For younger students, story tell the verses. At least read verses 2 and 3. Ask:]

- *Who is Jehoiakim?* [son of King Josiah, been king of Judah for four years]
- *What did God tell Jeremiah to do?* [Jeremiah was to write on a scroll all of the words that God had spoken against Israel, Judah, and all the nations.]
- *What did God hope would happen?* [He hoped the people of Judah would hear God's grievances against them and turn from their wicked ways so God could forgive them.]

Jeremiah obeyed God and had Baruch write down on a scroll all of the words he spoke. Once finished, Jeremiah, who was unable to go to the temple (possibly because of his unpopular speeches there; see Jer. 7:1–15 and 26:1–19), had Baruch take the scroll to the temple. On a day when the people were fasting, Baruch was to stand in the temple and read the scroll out loud in the hearing of everyone.

Baruch had to wait about nine months until a day of fasting took place.

(At this point in Jewish history, days of fasting were only called by the leadership during times of national emergency; see 2 Chronicles 20:3 and Joel 1:14, 2:15. Regular days of fasting were instituted after the fall of Jerusalem. Babylonian records tell us that Nebuchadnezzar captured the city of Ashkelon the same month as this fast. It is possible the leadership called a fast to plead for God's deliverance from Babylon.)

Then Baruch read the scroll at the New Gate. The scribes and the people heard him.

Micaiah, a son of one of the scribes, went to the king's house where all of the princes, or officials, were sitting. He told them everything he heard from Baruch. The officials sent for Baruch to hear the words for themselves. After

Baruch finished reading the scroll, the princes looked at each other in fear. The officials knew they had to tell the king.

They took the scroll, left it with the scribes, and told Baruch to go hide himself and Jeremiah because Jehoiakim would probably get very angry. The officials went to the king. Jehudi went to get the scroll and began to read the words to the king. The words were written vertically on the scroll, so as Jehudi finished reading three or four columns of words, the king took a knife and cut off the portion that had been read. He then threw the words into the fire.

The king had no remorse. He disregarded the words of God. Instead, King Jehoiakim ordered the arrest of Jeremiah and Baruch. God hid them both from the king's men.

LIFE APPLICATION

[Show the optical illusion. Ask:]

- *Who should have been asked for the directions on how to create this?* [you]
- *Who should we go to when we have problems in life?* [God]
- *Where do we find God's words?* [the Bible]
- *When we hear God's words how should we respond to them?* [Sometimes God's words are happy and filled with blessings; other times God's words hold warnings. Depending upon the Scripture we could respond with happiness, conviction, remorse, etc. But we should ALWAYS take God's word seriously.]
- *After we hear God's word, what should happen?* [This is a harder question. Guide children to James 1:22, which says that we should not just listen to the word of God, but then DO what it says.]
- *Did King Jehoiakim do what the scroll said to do?* [no]

[Hold up a sheet of paper and show the children how to do the illusion.]

Now I have shown you how to do this illusion. You have heard and seen the directions. Now if you do not go and DO the illusion for a friend or your parents, then showing you how to do this was of no value. This illusion is no fun if all you do is keep the information in your head. You have to go and DO this illusion so other people can join in on your fun.

The same thing goes with the Bible. The Bible is of no value if all you do is listen to it. You must do what it says! King Jehoiakim listened to God's word . . . but he DID NOT do what it said. Therefore, the kingdom of Judah would be captured by Babylon.

What is God saying through Jeremiah and King Jehoiakim? God takes sin and rebellion seriously. We can read and know what the Bible says, but if we do not DO what the Bible says to do, then our faith is not active.

What God is Saying

COMMENT BOX

■ ■ ■ ■ ■ ■ ■ ■ ■ ■ ■ ■ ■ ■ ■ ■ ■ ■ ■ ■

THINK: What went well as you taught this lesson? What can you do better?

_____
_____
_____
_____
_____
_____
_____
_____
_____

TIP: Teach the JumpStart3 scripture song for James 1:22. Also, check in with the children to see to whom they showed the illusion.

23 HABAKKUK QUESTIONS GOD

Children need to know that they can bring any questions and doubts to God. Use this Habakkuk lesson and activity to strengthen that understanding.

Scripture Focus: Habakkuk 1:1–6, 13; 2:4, 20; 3:17–19

Materials:

- One index card for each child
- Pencils
- One quiet worship song to play in background
- Bulletin board with a 3–4 foot brown paper cross stapled to it (or use a piece of 1-inch x 2-inch wood and a few nails to create a wooden cross)
- Push pins (bulletin board option)
- Small tack nails and hammer (for wooden cross option)

Geography: Southern Kingdom of Judah between 606–604 B.C. near the time when Babylon won the Battle of Carchemish (605 B.C.)

Background: Habakkuk is a different prophetic book. Instead of receiving a message

from God to take to the people, Habakkuk and God have a conversation about the people of Judah.

Judah was in its last days of "freedom." Good King Josiah died and his son Jehoahaz was on the throne. Within three months, Egypt invaded, took Jehoahaz off the throne, and put his brother Jehoiakim on the throne. Jehoiakim was not a godly man.

In the surrounding communities of Judah there was violence, inner turmoil, and greed. The Babylonians were rebelling against Assyria, and battles were fought. International relations were chaotic, and the people of Judah were living lives that reeked of individual pleasure and wickedness.

Preparation:

Bulletin Board Option: Use brown paper to create a cross about 3–4 feet in height; attach it to the bulletin board.

Wooden Cross Option: Cut the wood into 2 pieces so that you can nail them together to create a cross about 4 feet tall.

OBJECT LESSON

[Give out one index card and pencil to each child. Say:]

Imagine you are having a conversation with God, face to face. Perhaps this conversation takes place at breakfast or lunch. God looks at you and asks, *"If you could ask me anything, what question would you ask?"*

[Direct the children to think seriously about what they would ask God while you play one quiet worship song. Then have them write the question on the index card. Have them put their name on the card and then give it to you. Hold on to the cards until the activity at the end of this lesson.]

What God is Saying

BIBLE LESSON

The prophet Habakkuk had a conversation with God. Habakkuk asked God two questions.

[Read Habakkuk 1:1–6. Ask:]

- *What is the main question Habakkuk asks God in verses 2-4?* [Habakkuk asked God how long He was going to tolerate looking at all of the violence and strife in Judah. Was He ignoring it? Habakkuk was seeing God's people filled with greed, evil, injustice, and selfishness.]
- *What is the first thing God says for Habakkuk to do in verses 5-6?* [look and watch]
- *What was Habakkuk supposed to look and watch for?* [God was going to do a work which Habakkuk would not believe.]
- *What was God going to do?* [He was going to raise up the Chaldeans (Babylonians), and they were going to come and take dwellings (homes) that were not theirs.]
- *How did God describe the Babylonians?* [He said they were a bitter and hasty nation marching through the earth; pull in some adjectives from Habakkuk 1:7–11, if you choose: terrible, dreadful, violent, scoffing, offensive, worship idols.]
- *What was God's plan to bring justice for the evil of Judah?* [God was going to have the Babylonians take over Judah, and the people would become captives.]

Habakkuk asked God how could He stand to look and watch the evil and violence that His people were doing.

God answered by telling Habakkuk that He was going to allow the Babylonians to conquer Judah as punishment for their evil choices.

This answer did not sit well with Habakkuk. He really was shocked and had a hard time believing what God told him. Therefore, Habakkuk proceeded to ask God another question.

[Read Habakkuk 1:13 and 2:4, 20. Ask:]

- *How does Habakkuk describe God in verse 13?* [pure eyes; cannot look at wickedness]
- *What question does Habakkuk ask?* [If God is holy and pure, how can God look at the evilness of the Babylonians and use them to punish His people of Judah who were more righteous? Even though the people of Judah were acting evil, Habakkuk still saw them as more righteous than the Gentile Babylonians.]
- *How does God answer in Habakkuk 2:4?* [He called the Babylonians proud, or conceited, and said that they would eventually fall; the righteous, or just, however, would live by faith.]
- *What do we learn about God in verse 20?* [He is in His temple; all the earth should be silent before Him.]
- *What does that mean?* [God is holy; we are not. Who are we to question how God goes about this earth? God is always at work around us, even when we do not understand.]

Habakkuk asked really hard questions! How could a holy God watch His righteous people be destroyed and taken captive by an evil nation?

God is a God of answers. Even the strong, evil nation of Babylon will fall to destruction one day.

"Living by faith" had a slightly different meaning in the Old Testament. In the Old Testament the people of Israel and Judah were waiting for the Messiah, the King of Justice, to come. A good righteous Israelite would stay true to God's law and live a humble life of waiting. He would enjoy God's provisions and security. A person of faith would fully rely on God and trust in Him.

"Living by faith" for New Testament believers, and us today, would mean living a life that reflects Jesus while waiting for Him to return a second time.

When Habakkuk heard God's answer and heard that God would eventually bring about Babylon's destruction, he responded with a prayer.

LIFE APPLICATION

[Read Habakkuk 3:17–19. Ask:]

- *What bad things are described by Habakkuk?* [no figs, no grapes, no olives, no flocks or herds]
- *Why would these terrible things to have happen?* [The fruit, flocks, and herds were examples of the main ways the people of Judah would have lived; these were how they would have gotten food and money.]
- *What was Habakkuk going to do anyway?* [rejoice in the Lord]
- *How does Habakkuk describe God?* [He describes God as his salvation and his strength.]
- *To what does Habakkuk compare himself?* [a mountain deer which was sure-footed and able to walk in rocky mountains with confidence]

Having peace in our lives does not depend upon our outer circumstances. Habakkuk listed terrible things that would have cost the livelihood of the people of Judah; however, he chose to rejoice in the Lord anyway. God is the source of our joy.

Our satisfaction in life comes from God and from nowhere else. Many people try different things other than God to bring joy. Those things will not work. They might make a person happy for a moment, but not truly joyful. Joy is from the Holy Spirit.

Habakkuk praised God and said that God was his salvation and strength. Habakkuk knew anything could happen to him. In any case, his trust would be in God and no where else.

[Give back the index cards. Ask:]

- *I am going to give you your card back. Do you want to add a new question for God?* [Allow children to add to their questions.]

[Turn the quiet music on again. As they finish, tell the children to bring

their cards to you. Give them a push pin or a nail to "nail" their questions to the cross of Jesus. Once all questions have been placed, say:]

God is the only One who knows the answers to all questions. It is OK to go to Him when you have a question or when you have doubts about anything.

God knew you would have questions. He sent Jesus to earth to answer some of those questions. One question that Jesus answered was, *"Who is the long-awaited Messiah?"*

We already know Jesus has come! He is our strength. Jesus brings us joy.

What is God saying through Habakkuk? It is normal to have questions. We should take them to God through prayer and see how He answers. Sometimes His answers might confuse us, but God is trustworthy, faithful, and worthy of our praise.

COMMENT BOX

THINK: What went well as you taught this lesson? What can you do better?

_____
_____
_____
_____
_____
_____
_____
_____
_____

TIP: After the children are gone, take down the questions and read through them. You might find some great questions to focus on during your next Bible teaching class!

24 DANIEL AND THE WRITING ON THE WALL

God searches our hearts (1 Chronicles 28:9; Romans 8:27). Use this lesson to show how two hearts measured up to God's standards.

Scripture Focus: Daniel 5

Materials:

- Paper
- Lemon juice (fresh if possible)
- Cotton swab (like a Q-tip)
- Typing paper
- Votive candle in a holder or on a plate (any candle will work, though)
- Scale (a balance would be best)
- Fire safety equipment (just in case!)

Geography: Babylon

Background: Even though the book of Daniel is placed with the books of the prophets, Daniel himself never claimed to be a prophet. Jesus was the One who called Daniel a prophet (Matthew 24:15).

"I have heard that you are able to explain what things mean. And you can find the answers to hard problems. Read this writing on the wall and explain it to me."
— Daniel 5:16 (ICB)

Daniel was taken captive by Nebuchadnezzar (605 B.C.) and sent to Babylon. We know that he was young when he was taken, handsome, and intelligent (Daniel 1:3, 6). We also know that he at least lived until the third year of King Cyrus, which would have been 536 B.C.

Daniel is the first great apocalyptic book. "Apocalyptic" refers to an unveiling, or revelation. Some apocalyptic Scripture was revealed through visions. Other Scripture uses signs or symbols. Another trait of apocalyptic Scripture is the use of prose, or ordinary language, instead of poetry. Most of the time apocalyptic Scripture describes future events and must be carefully compared to other Scriptures for interpretations.

Preparation: Before the lesson, create your secret message. Squeeze the lemon juice or use lemon juice from a bottle. Dip the cotton swab into the juice. Use the swab to write the words MENE, MENE, TEKEL, UPHARSIN. Let it dry.

OBJECT LESSON

[Show the paper.]

There is a secret message on this paper. Can you read it?

[Show both sides of the paper. The paper might be wrinkled from the dry juice, but the students should not be able to read the message.]

I am going to use this candle to help us read the message.

[Light the candle. With the juice side up, carefully hold the paper over the flame (not in it) so the heat can cause the juice to burn slightly and reveal the letters. Practice this before your lesson so you do not burn your building down.]

Now we can read the message: Mene (me-ne, short *e* for both), Tekel (te-kl, short *e*), Upharsin (oo-far-sin, short *a* and *i*). Hmmm . . . I wonder what this means?

BIBLE LESSON

[Ask:]

- *What do you know about Daniel?* [Use this question as a review. Possible answers include: Daniel and friends not eating the food of the king; Daniel having a dream or vision about a huge statue; Daniel and the lions' den.]

[Read Daniel 5. This is a long passage. Consider breaking it up and asking questions as you go. Ask:]

- *Who is having a feast?* [King Belshazzar of Babylon and 1,000 of his lords]
- *What does the king decide to do?* [to bring out the gold and silver vessels from the Jerusalem temple to use for drinking wine during the feast]
- *What did the king see?* [The fingers of a man's hand appeared and wrote a message on the wall.]
- *How did the king respond?* [He was terrified; his hip joints loosened and his knees knocked (a commentary said this is a nice way of saying that he lost control of his bowels).]
- *For whom did the king call?* [the astrologers and wise men]
- *When the wise men could not decipher the message, how did the king respond?* [terror; his countenance changed]
- *How did the queen respond?* [She reminded the king about Daniel. Because she was not at the feast, and because of the short history lesson she gave to Belshazzar, Bible scholars think the queen was his mother.]
- *How did she describe Daniel?* [The Spirit of the Holy God was in him; wisdom and understanding were in him; chief of the magicians, astrologers, Chaldeans, and soothsayers; had an excellent spirit and understanding; interpreted dreams, solved riddles, and explained enigmas]

Daniel and the Writing on the Wall

- *Daniel gave the king another history lesson about Nebuchadnezzar. Of what did he accuse the king?* [He did not have a humble heart even though he knew all of the history that happened with his grandfather, Nebuchadnezzar; he lifted himself against God by using the temple's vessels; he praised idols instead of God. (Daniel 5:22)]
- *How does Daniel describe God?* [holds our breath and owns all our ways]
- *Do you remember God's answer to Habakkuk about Babylon?* [Allow for answers; see Habakkuk lesson.]

Daniel was able to interpret the message.

[Hold up the message and read the words as you explain their meanings.]

MENE: The weight of 50 shekels (1¼ pounds). God had numbered Belshazzar's kingdom.

TEKEL: This refers to one shekel (2/5 of an ounce). God had weighed Belshazzar and he was found wanting, or not enough.

UPHARSIN: This means to break in two. Daniel told the king that his kingdom was going to be divided by the Medes and Persians.

That very night Belshazzar was killed, and Darius of Persia became the new king.

LIFE APPLICATION

[Bring out the scale. Ask:]

- *Have you ever weighed anything before?* [Allow for answers. They will probably answer yes.]
- *Have you ever had a parent or authority figure count down to get your attention to obey, or to do something?* [Allow for answers.]

God had been watching Belshazzar. God had been numbering his days, or counting down, until Belshazzar must be punished for his corruption and disobedience.

God had weighed Belshazzar, not physically, but spiritually. God weighed the king's heart.

[For older children who are studying, or have studied, ancient history: Some ancient religions believed that when a person died, the god of the dead would weigh their heart. If the heart was light, then the dead person could go to the afterlife. If the heart was heavy, then the person would be banished, or eaten by the god.]

God weighed the heart of Belshazzar, and it was found wanting, which meant something was missing. His heart was not right. Instead, it was corrupt and evil.

Daniel then predicted that the kingdom would be overtaken and split. This did happen.

[Ask:]

- *Remember how the queen described Daniel?* [The Spirit of the Holy God is in him; wisdom and understanding were in him. He was made chief of the magicians, astrologers, Chaldeans, and soothsayers. He had an excellent spirit and understanding. He interpreted dreams, solved riddles, and explained enigmas.]
- *Are there people who can describe you that way?* [Allow for answers.]

- *If God were to weigh your heart, what would He find?* [Allow for answers.]
- *What do we know about our spiritual hearts?* [Read Jeremiah 17:9–10; discuss that the Lord searches all hearts, just like He did with Belshazzar; God also gives according to what He finds, or the ways of the heart.]
- *How can we have hearts that are not wanting?* [We must believe in Jesus with our whole hearts.]

Daniel exhibited characteristics that showed other people that he lived God's way. Daniel had a whole heart for God and the Gentile Babylonian Queen knew it.

You can be like Daniel, and not like Belshazzar.

Jesus explained that He Himself was the only way to get to the Father. If God searches your heart and finds Jesus there, then eternal life is yours.

What is God saying through Daniel? People who rebel against God will be found wanting, but those who choose to believe in Jesus with a whole heart will have eternal life.

COMMENT BOX

■ ■ ■ ■ ■ ■ ■ ■ ■ ■ ■ ■ ■ ■ ■ ■ ■ ■ ■ ■

THINK: What went well as you taught this lesson? What can you do better?

_____
_____
_____
_____
_____
_____
_____
_____
_____

TIP: Teach the students the song "Dare to be a Daniel." You can find the song and lyrics on the Resources Page.

25 EZEKIEL AND THE DRY BONES

What do dry bones and two sticks have to do with Jesus? Use this lesson to teach children that God is trustworthy and that new life comes through Jesus.

Scripture Focus: Ezekiel 37

Materials:

- Poster of a skeleton (even better if you have a Halloween skeleton with the body parts that move)
- Two sticks or dowel rods
- Paper to make a red flag for Judah and a blue flag for Israel (write the name on each color and attach one to each stick)
- String, Velcro strip, or rubber band to put the sticks together

Geography: Babylon; 593 B.C.

Background: Along with Jeremiah and Zechariah, Ezekiel was a priest. Because of this, Ezekiel focused much of his writing on the temple and the glory of God. Scholars think that Ezekiel was 30 years old when his ministry began (Ezekiel 1:1); his ministry lasted about 22 years.

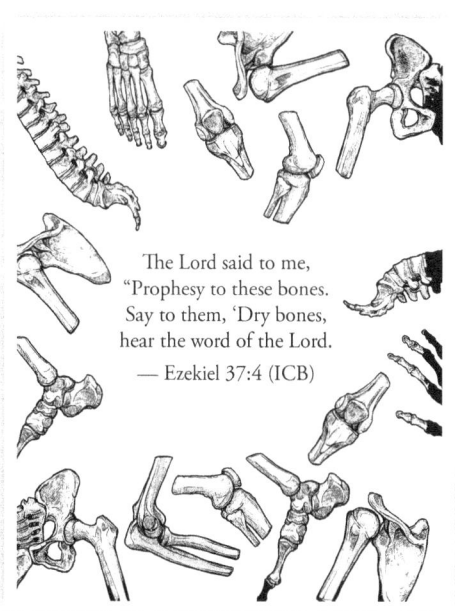

The Lord said to me, "Prophesy to these bones. Say to them, 'Dry bones, hear the word of the Lord.
— Ezekiel 37:4 (ICB)

This book was written when Judah was in bondage by Babylon. Ezekiel lived near the Kebar River in Babylon. The first part of Ezekiel's book focuses on the destruction of Jerusalem. Nobody believed him. After Jerusalem was destroyed, Ezekiel focused on the restoration of Israel.

OBJECT LESSON

[Read Ezekiel 37:1. Ask:]

- *Have you ever had a really strange or scary dream?* [Allow for answers. Take a few minutes to share dreams.]

Ezekiel had a strange dream as well. He had a dream that took him to a valley, or a plain. It was filled with bones. They were scattered everywhere.

[Show the skeleton.]

- *What is this?* [a skeleton]
- *Where do we find real skeletons?* [inside bodies of animals and humans]
- *How do you think Ezekiel felt when he saw all of those bones in his dream?* [He may have felt scared, nervous, or curious about what God would tell him.]

Here are some fun facts that I bet you do not know about your bones:

1. Adults usually have 206 bones, but babies are born with 300!
2. Half of your bones are found in your hands and feet.
3. There is only one bone that is not connected to another bone in your body. The hyoid is a bone that is surrounded by muscles just under the base of your tongue.

Ezekiel and the Dry Bones

BIBLE LESSON

In Ezekiel's dream, there were a lot of bones, and they were dry like they had been sitting there for a while. In the dream God asked Ezekiel, *"Do you think these bones live?"* Not knowing how to answer that question, Ezekiel stated, *"You know."*

[Read Ezekiel 37:4–14. Ask:]

- *What was Ezekiel to prophesy over the bones?* [Hear the word of the Lord. The Lord will cause breath to enter them, and they will live.]
- *What were the bones to know about God?* [that He is the Lord]
- *What happened after Ezekiel spoke to the bones?* [The bones rattled and started fitting together. Then the muscles and skin were added, but they did not have any breath.]
- *To what was Ezekiel to prophesy next?* [to the breath]
- *What was the prophecy?* [The breath was to come from the four winds and breathe on the dead bones so they could live.]
- *What happened after Ezekiel prophesied?* [The breath entered them, and they stood up. There was a great army.]
- *What do the bones represent?* [the entire house of Israel; Judah and Israel]
- *Why did the people of Israel say that they had dry bones and no hope?* [They had been exiled and were away from their land and people.]
- *What prophecy was Ezekiel to give them?* [God will open the graves of the Jews and bring them back to their land. He will place His Spirit in them, and they will live.]

[Show the two sticks. Storytell Ezekiel 37:15–28. Act it out with the sticks.]

God came to Ezekiel again. He told Ezekiel to get two sticks. On one he was to write the word *Judah*, for that kingdom. On the other one he was to write the word *Israel*. Then Ezekiel joined the two sticks together, and they became one. God was telling Ezekiel that He was going to bring people from the Kingdom of Israel and from the Kingdom of Judah and unite them again. He would become their God once again. Then He goes on to say that one King will rule over them all. He will be a Shepherd from the line of David. A new covenant will be made—an everlasting covenant. God ended by telling Ezekiel that He will tabernacle, or dwell, with His people.

LIFE APPLICATION

What does this strange dream have to do with us? First, it is important for us to understand that if God says He is going to do something, then we can trust His word. God is incapable of lying and this makes Him trustworthy.

The other thing we need to understand is that God loves His people, the Jews. God also loves gentiles who choose to believe in Jesus!

Remember what God told Ezekiel to prophesy over the wind?

[Reread Ezekiel 37:14. Ask:]

- *When the disciples received the Holy Spirit at Pentecost, what sound did they hear?* [It was a mighty rushing wind.]

When a person decides to believe in Jesus, the Holy Spirit begins to dwell inside of them. God begins to tabernacle, to dwell, with that person.

An old life is covered in sin, death, and darkness. An old life before Jesus looks like a bunch of old, dry bones. A new life in Jesus looks like an army of live people filled with the wind of the Holy Spirit.

This prophecy has not totally happened yet. It has been fulfilled for the Gentiles, but not to the Jews. This prophecy seems to be talking about Jews who choose to believe in Jesus and therefore have the Spirit of God dwelling inside of them just like Gentile believers.

In Romans 11, Paul talks about how the Gentiles were saved through Jesus so that some of the Jews would then be saved through Jesus.

Therefore, it is important for us to get to know our Jewish friends. Get to know what they think about Jesus. Have conversations about Jesus with them. You never know, maybe you can help lead a Jewish person to Christ!

What is God saying through Ezekiel and the dry bones? God will always do what He says He will do even if we do not actually see it happen in our lifetime. God wants to take the dry bones of our spirit and bring them to life with the Holy Spirit. That will happen through faith in Jesus Christ.

What God is Saying

COMMENT BOX

■ ■ ■ ■ ■ ■ ■ ■ ■ ■ ■ ■ ■ ■ ■ ■ ■

THINK: What went well as you taught this lesson? What can you do better?

_____
_____
_____
_____
_____
_____
_____
_____
_____

TIP: If you have a Jewish synagogue in your area, consider contacting them to see if you can do a children's activity together, or have a guest speaker come to your group to learn about the Jewish people.

26 HAGGAI AND THE REBUILDING OF THE TEMPLE

The Jews returned to their beloved Jerusalem and had begun to rebuild the temple. Use the discouragement of the Jews and God's encouragement to remind children that God has a plan for their lives.

Scripture Focus: Haggai 2:1–9

Materials:

- 1 complete plastic brick set in a box with a picture of the completed project on the outside (a castle or other big building would be especially good for this). Use a picture if needed. You can easily find a picture from the website.
- Random plastic bricks in bags or open bins (one container per 4–5 children; use fewer bricks than what are needed to build the brick project pictured)

Geography: Jerusalem in approximately 520 B.C., after the return from exile in Babylon

Background: Haggai prophesied for only four months during the time of the rebuilding of the temple in Jerusalem. In his book he mentions twenty-five times that the words

I made a promise to you when you came out of Egypt. My Spirit is still with you. So don't be afraid.
— Haggai 2:5 (ICB)

he spoke were from the Lord Almighty. This tells us that Haggai knew he was a prophet of God.

It is possible that Haggai was one of those exiled to Babylon, because he mentions the splendor of Solomon's temple that had been destroyed. If this is true, then Haggai would have been an old man.

King Darius the Great of Persia allowed the Jews to go back and rebuild their temple and homeland. Haggai was the first prophet to bring a message from God after the Exile. The message he brought to the people was that they needed to *"give careful thought to their ways."* They had been in their homeland for sixteen years and had stopped working on the temple in order to build beautiful homes for themselves. God told them that now was the time to finish rebuilding the temple. The people responded in obedience and immediately began to work on the temple. It was completed in 515 B.C.

Haggai and the Rebuilding of the Temple

OBJECT LESSON

[Show the completed brick box picture and the containers of bricks. Say:]

Look at the box. You can see on the outside of the box the picture of what it is supposed to look like when we build it.

[Point out some of the details of the project. Have the children get into groups of 3–5. Give each group a container of plastic bricks. Place the picture where everyone can see it. Say:]

Your job is to try to build this project as best you can with the plastic bricks that you have been given. You have fifteen minutes to work together to get as much done as you can.

[Allow the children to work on their projects. Walk around and encourage them. Let them know how much time they have left every few minutes. Count down the final seconds. *"10-9-8-7-6-5-4-3-2-1—everybody stop!"* **Ask:]**

- *Tell me what you think of your project. Do you think it turned out like the project on the box?* [Allow for answers. Guide the children to understand that they did not have all the bricks they needed to complete the project to look like the one on the box. In fact, they did not have the correct bricks needed to build the project.]

In 586 B.C. the Babylonians had destroyed Jerusalem. They destroyed the temple where God was worshipped and led the people off to be slaves in Babylon. Eventually, the king of Persia conquered Babylon and allowed the Jews to go back to Judah. He allowed the people to begin rebuilding the city and the temple.

The people who had come back to Jerusalem tried to rebuild the temple to look like the one that had been destroyed. They did not have the resources to build it like King Solomon did. They did not have enough people to do the work. They did not have the silver, gold, and precious jewels with which the temple had been decorated. They did not have the money to purchase those beautiful things. They looked at what they had built, and the people who had seen the temple back in the day were so sad, because the one they had built looked pitiful by comparison.

[Read Haggai 2:1-9. Ask:]

- *To whom is Haggai giving this message from God?* [Zerubbabel, the governor; Joshua, the high priest; and the remnant of the people]
- *Haggai asked three questions. What were they?* [1. Who saw Solomon's temple and its glory? 2. How does that temple look now? And 3. Does it not seem as nothing?]

[Show the original structure picture.]

This is what you were striving to create. It is a beautiful building. But your creations do not look like it much at all.

[Ask:]

- *How do you feel about your building versus the original one you wanted to make?* [Allow for answers. Discuss their disappointment or frustration.]

The Jews felt the same way. They knew they could not rebuild their new temple to be like the magnificent one Solomon built.

God gave them amazing encouragement.

[Ask:]

- *What does God say three times?* [Be strong.]
- *To what historical time does God refer?* [the Exodus from Egypt when Moses led the people out of slavery]

God reminded the Jews about how He was with their ancestors when they came out of slavery from Egypt. God encouraged the leaders and the people that He was still with them. His Spirit was still among them.

He told them not to worry about not being able to make the temple as rich and glorious as it used to be.

[Ask:]

- *What will God do once more?* [He will shake heaven and earth; when Jesus returns the second time the earth and sky will tremble. (Matthew 24:29–30)]
- *What does God say about a future temple?* [This temple would be filled with glory; silver and gold belong to God; the glory of the future temple will be greater than Solomon's temple; it would be filled with peace.]
- *Why do you think this future temple will be filled with glory?* [Jesus will be there. (Luke 2:29–32)]

The temple the Jewish exiles built would eventually be expanded by King Herod. It was magnificent, but still not as wonderful as Solomon's temple.

The Herodian temple would be the temple Jesus would visit. Jesus walked and talked, taught people, healed people, and glorified God in the temple. One of the names of Jesus is Prince of Peace.

In AD 70 the Herodian temple was destroyed by Rome. It has not been rebuilt.

Jesus is full of God's grace, truth, and glory. One day the earth will shake, and Jesus will return to Jerusalem. A new temple will be built. Haggai tells us that nations will come to *"the Desire,"* the Messiah, of all nations.

LIFE APPLICATION

■■■■■■■■■■■■■■■■■■

[Ask:]

- *What does it mean to compare?* [Allow for answers. Discuss how the Jews compared the old temple with the new temple and were sad because it did not measure up in their eyes. Discuss that God sees things differently than us. For example, the Lord looks at the heart (1 Samuel 16:7).]
- *Do you compare yourself to others? If so, to whom?* [Possible answers include their friends, sports figures, social media influencers, YouTubers, etc.]

[Show the unopened project box. Say:]

God gives us all the pieces we need to do whatever He has planned for our lives. When you compare, it is like you are trying to use the pieces of someone else's project to build your life.

We have to look to God to see what He wants for our daily lives and our future. He's the one who has the box with the picture on it, so to speak. That means He knows what His good plans are for you, and how it will ultimately build your life. Comparing your life with others is the same as telling God His plans are not good enough! But God says, *"For I know the plans I have for you, plans to prosper you and not to harm you, plans to give you hope and a future."* (Jeremiah 29:11)

God knows you better than anyone else. God loves you more than anyone else. You can trust His plans for you. He knows what your life is meant to look like.

What is God saying through Haggai? Just as God encouraged the Jews to rebuild the temple, He encourages us to be strong in Him and to remember that He will be with us always, even to the end of the age.

COMMENT BOX

THINK: What went well as you taught this lesson? What can you do better?

_____
_____
_____
_____
_____
_____
_____
_____
_____
_____

TIP: This is a great lesson to use maps and drawings of Solomon's temple and the Herodian temple. See the Resources Page. Discuss the differences and similarities.

27 ZECHARIAH AND THE TEMPLE

■■■■■■■■■■■■■■■■

Why is the temple so important? Use this lesson to teach children about rebuilding the Jerusalem temple and how God dwells with us today.

Scripture Focus: Zechariah 1:1–6; 2:1–5, 10–11; 9:9

Materials:

- Measuring tape

Geography: Babylon and Jerusalem before 515 B.C. while the temple was being rebuilt

Background: Zechariah was a Levite who was born in Babylon. In 539 B.C., King Cyrus of Persia issued a declaration allowing the Jews in captivity to return to their homeland. Zechariah, along with 50,000 other Jews, returned to Israel. Most probably went to Jerusalem.

"Shout and be glad, Jerusalem. I am coming, and I will live among you," says the Lord.
— Zechariah 2:10 (ICB)

Zerubbabel was the governor, and Joshua was the high priest. They set about rebuilding the temple and getting the sacrificial offerings reinstituted. Over the next sixteen years, the building would drag on because of outsider interference and indifference by the Jews.

Zechariah and the Temple

God gave words to the prophet Haggai, who encouraged the Jews to keep on building the temple. Two months after Haggai stopped preaching, Zechariah began motivating the people. His ministry focused on urging the people to rebuild the temple because of God's future plan.

OBJECT LESSON

[Show the measuring tape. Say:]

This is a measuring tape. It is used in construction. When buildings are being created, a measuring tape is used to make sure the angles are straight and everything is measured correctly. It is a small tool, but very important.

[Ask:]

- *What might happen if a builder decided not to use a measuring tape?* [Allow for answers. The walls and foundation could be crooked, which would cause the building to not be square; the building could fall down.]

[Use the measuring tape to measure different items around the room, such as the door, window, table, book, etc.]

If we were building this room, then we must know the exact size of the door. If we were building a bookshelf, then we would want to make sure the book would fit. A measuring tape gives us information that we need.

Zechariah and the Temple

BIBLE LESSON

Zechariah was a prophet to the Jews after they were released from captivity in Babylon. King Cyrus of Persia had taken over Babylon and allowed the Jews to go home. About 50,000 Jews returned to Israel.

The Jews had been back in Jerusalem for fifteen years and were still trying to rebuild a new temple. Outsiders were distracting them from the work. The Jews were not caring about the work either.

As we read Zechariah's words to the Jews, listen for the measuring tape, or measuring line. Also, try to count the times you hear the words *"Lord of Hosts."*

[Read Zechariah 1:1–6. Ask:]

- *Who was the king?* [The king was Darius of Persia. This is significant because Zechariah was reminding the Jews that a son of David was NOT on the throne of Israel.]
- *What do we learn about the Lord?* [He had been angry with the fathers of the Jews (the generations before the captivity); He wanted the people to return to Him, and then He will return to them]
- *What does God remind the people about their fathers?* [The former prophets told them to turn from their evil ways, but they did not listen; they were disobedient.]

Zechariah is reminding the Jews about how their fathers did not listen to the prophets God sent to them. Instead, they turned from God and did what was evil. Because of this, God did exactly what He said He would do.

It is important to remember past mistakes because we can learn from them. This was what Zechariah wanted the Jews to do. God was at work, and Zechariah wanted them to get their focus back on God.

God gave Zechariah eight visions. We are going to learn about one of them.

What God is Saying

[Read Zechariah 2:1–5, 10–11. Ask:]

- *Who did Zechariah see?* [a man with a measuring line]
- *What was the man doing?* [measuring Jerusalem]
- *What do we learn about Jerusalem?* [It will one day have towns without walls because there will be many people and livestock.]
- *How will Jerusalem be protected?* [The Lord will be a wall of fire around it; His glory will be in the center.]
- *Who is coming?* [the Lord]
- *What is He going to do?* [dwell in Israel]
- *What things are going to happen in that day?* [Many nations will join to the Lord; they will be God's people; God will dwell with them.]

[Hold up the measuring tape. Say:]

Wow. This is quite the vision! A man who had a measuring line was measuring Jerusalem. Bible scholars think this meant that God was checking to see if Jerusalem was "straight" or perfectly lined up with His ways. The temple needed to be built so the people could worship God in the ways He had told Moses and Israel way back in history.

God wanted Jerusalem to be righteous because He was coming. He was going to dwell in the land. Because of God coming, somehow, nations were going to choose Him to be their God.

Zechariah and the Temple

LIFE APPLICATION

[Read Zechariah 9:9. Ask:]

- *What does this verse tell us about the King who is coming to Jerusalem?* [He is just, has salvation, is lowly, and will ride a donkey.]

Zechariah, over 400 years before Jesus walked the earth, told the Jews that their Messiah would be coming to dwell, or live, in Israel. Up to this point in history, God either dwelled in the tabernacle or the temple. Dwelling among the people was a strange thought. Not only was God going to dwell among the people of Israel, but He was going to bring salvation to Israel and other nations.

Jesus did exactly what Zechariah foretold. He was lowly. He was humble. Jesus did ride the colt of a donkey into Jerusalem. All of the Jewish leaders would have known these verses from Zechariah. Instead of recognizing Jesus as the Messiah, they accused Him of blasphemy. Blasphemy means they accused Him of claiming to be equal with God.

Zechariah 9:9 told Israel to rejoice greatly and shout when the King entered Jerusalem. If you remember the event, when Jesus entered Jerusalem on the donkey, the people shouted and waved palm branches. They were excited!

Then they were confused. Jesus, the One they thought was the Messiah, died on a cross. Jesus brought salvation from sin, not salvation from oppressing nations.

Because of Jesus, you can be one of those people who dwells with God that are described in Zechariah 2:11. One day, many nations of people will join together to worship and dwell with the King!

What is God saying through Zechariah? The Jews needed to finish building the temple because God had a plan to dwell among His people. They needed to learn from the mistakes of their fathers and look forward to the King that was to come.

What God is Saying

COMMENT BOX

■■■■■■■■■■■■■■■■■■■

THINK: What went well as you taught this lesson? What can you do better?

_____
_____
_____
_____
_____
_____
_____
_____
_____

TIP: Bring in other types of measuring tools such as rulers, meter sticks, a scale, etc. Allow the children to measure items in the room.

28 MALACHI PROPHESIES THE COMING MESSIAH

God could be sarcastic at times when He was scolding the Israelites. Use this lesson to listen to God's charges against His people and hear God's message of hope for the future.

Scripture Focus: Malachi 1:6–8, 3:1, 4:1–5

Materials:

- Calendar
- Clock
- Envelope
- Piece of white paper

Geography: Jerusalem and Judah

Background: Malachi was the last Old Testament prophet. He prophesied about 100 years after the Israelites were permitted to return home to Israel from Babylon. God had been faithful to the Israelites, but once again they had proved to be unfaithful to Him. Life was hard. Persia was now in charge, and there had been many locusts and bad crops. Malachi encouraged the people that their faithfulness would bring about blessing.

The Lord of heaven's armies says, "I will send my messenger. He will prepare the way for me to come. Suddenly, the Lord you are looking for will come to his Temple. The messenger of the agreement, whom you want, will come."
— Malachi 3:1 (ICB)

However, the people doubted God was going to save them. They became indifferent toward worship by offering unworthy sacrifices of lame, ill, or blemished animals. They also refused to tithe, or contribute a tenth to the temple.

After Malachi there were 400 years of silence before Jesus was born. Jesus would fulfill the Law and the prophets.

Preparation: Write Malachi 3:1 on the sheet of white paper. Fold the paper and place it inside the envelope.

OBJECT LESSON

[Show the envelope. Say:]

The messages of the prophets have been like letters to the people from God. The prophet Malachi was no different. The people had once again become indifferent toward God. They were offering blemished or sick animals for sacrifices instead of the animals without blemish. The people were marrying Gentiles and then divorcing. They neglected people and were disobedient to God in many ways.

Yet God had one final message for His people.

[Have a volunteer open the letter and read the verse. Ask:]

- *Think about everything you have learned about the prophets. What do you think this verse means?* [Allow for answers. Write them on a white board to see if anyone is correct when you end the lesson.]

BIBLE LESSON

[Read Malachi 1:6–8. Ask:]

- *To what does God compare Himself and His people?* [son and father; servant and master]
- *What is said about the priests?* [They despised God's name.]
- *Of what are the Israelites guilty?* [They have offered defiled, or cast-off, food on God's altar; they have offered blemished, blind, lame, or sick sacrifices.]
- *What tone of voice does it sound like God is using?* [Allow for answers. He sounds like He is scolding and even being sarcastic with His questioning.]

A son looks up to and honors his father. A servant honors and obeys his master. God asked the people, *"Why are you not honoring and obeying Me?"* Even the priests, who were supposed to worship God in the temple and lead the people in righteousness, were accepting offerings that were blatantly against what God had originally commanded way back in history with Moses on Mt. Sinai.

God told the people to take the sick animals and offer them to their governor. He knew that the governor would not want the nasty meat.

Yet they were offering this to the Lord.

Malachi then proceeded to give the Israelites an important message.

[Read the verse on the paper again.]

God was going to send a messenger to the people. He was going to prepare the way before the Lord. The Lord would be going to the temple. Again, God told them that the messenger would be coming.

Malachi Prophesies the Coming Messiah

[Ask:]

- *Who do you think is the messenger?* [Allow for answers. Go over the list from earlier to see if any of the answers make sense; if you are teaching the lessons in order, do not tell the answer, but encourage them to come the next time to see if they are correct. Build anticipation!]

[Hold up the calendar and the clock. Ask:]

- *Have you ever had to use a calendar? Why?* [Allow for answers.]
- *Have you ever had to set a timer to help you wait?* [Allow for answers.]
- *Is it hard to wait sometimes?* [Allow for answers. Have them give examples illustrating having to wait.]

The Israelites had been waiting and waiting and waiting for the Messiah to come.

This was a super important message. God was going to send a messenger to Israel. Maybe the Messiah was about to come! That should have been so exciting!!

God had more to say, though, to His people. Remember, He was not happy with them. He wanted them to change their ways and worship Him with a whole heart.

[Read Malachi 4:1–5. Ask:]

- *What day is coming?* [One that burns like an oven; the proud and wicked will stumble.]
- *What other words have prophets used to describe this day?* [the day of the Lord]
- *What do we learn about another group of people?* [Those who fear God's name shall arise; they will be healed; they will grow fat (healthy); they will trample the wicked.]

LIFE APPLICATION

████████████████████████

God gave Malachi a message for the Israelites. Stop dishonoring God's name. Stop offering nasty, blemished animals for sacrifices. Stop living unrighteous lives. Stop treating people unfairly. Stop being prideful.

Instead, God wanted the people to live righteous lives. He wanted to be honored. He wanted them to obey His commands.

The people needed to be ready because He was going to send a messenger who was going to prepare the way for the Lord.

But remember, God warned the people through Malachi that the day of the Lord was going to come, too. It would be a day of final judgment against those who chose to dishonor or disobey God, and to live unrighteous lives.

This sounds like an awful day! It will be. However, God's message tells us that those who fear Him, or honor Him, and attempt to live righteous lives will have nothing to worry about.

That message is for us as well because the day of the Lord has not arrived yet. One day God is going to judge those who honor Him and those who do not. Those who have honored God by choosing Jesus as their Savior will be with God in His kingdom forever. Those who have dishonored God, chosen to push Jesus away, and live their own lives will be completely excluded from God's kingdom.

This is one reason why it is important for us to share about Jesus with people around us.

After Malachi's message, God did not speak through prophets for 400 years. This time period is called 400 Years of Silence. No words of God were written down. God was at work though.

Malachi Prophesies the Coming Messiah

[Hold up the calendar. Say:]

This calendar is for one year . . . just one year. It took 400 calendars to measure the time the Israelites would have to wait before God spoke again!

What is God saying through Malachi? The Israelites turned from God. Because of this they missed out on His blessings and received judgment. The same thing could happen to us. God gives us hope because those who choose to walk in God's ways and obey Him will be blessed by entering into God's kingdom forever.

COMMENT BOX

THINK: What went well as you taught this lesson? What can you do better?

_____
_____
_____
_____
_____
_____
_____
_____
_____

> **TIP:** This lesson might be too deep for younger children. Know your audience and adapt to meet their needs. However, it is good for children to know that they can either choose God or not choose God. Then you take the consequence of your choice.

29 JOHN THE BAPTIST: THE GREATEST PROPHET

A re we allowed to question God? Is God able to handle our questions? Use this lesson to discuss the time when John the Baptist, the greatest prophet, doubted and questioned Jesus.

Scripture Focus: Luke 7:18–28; Isaiah 61:1–2

Materials:

- Edible crickets or grasshoppers, any flavor (You do not have to eat them, but you might have a student or two take you up on the offer!)
- Cups and water to wash down the crickets

Geography: Area in Galilee during Jesus' ministry

Background: Jesus had a cousin who was six months older than He was. His name was John. John had a ministry that took place near the Jordan River. He called people to repent and told them that the kingdom of God was coming, just like the prophets of the Old Testament.

One day Jesus came to John and was baptized. John announced that Jesus was the Lamb of God who takes away the sins of the world.

In the process of calling people out of sin, John made people mad at him. John ended up in jail. John knew that Jesus was the Messiah; however, in his dark days in jail, even he doubted sometimes.

But what did you go out to see? A prophet?
Yes, and I tell you, John is more than a prophet.
This was written about John:
'I will send my messenger ahead of you.
He will prepare the way for you.'
— Luke 7:26-27 (ICB)

What God is Saying

OBJECT LESSON

[Show the edible crickets or grasshoppers. Say:]

Look at these! People in different cultures around the world will eat crickets or grasshoppers. It is a normal food for them.

[Ask:]

- *Anyone want to try one?* [Allow for a few volunteers. Have them each try a cricket and describe how it tastes. You are welcome to try one as well!]

BIBLE LESSON

Jesus considered John the Baptist to be the greatest prophet.

John the Baptist was strange. He lived in the desert, wore animal skins, and ate honey and locusts. Crickets and grasshoppers are similar to locusts.

John's ministry lasted about one year. He called out to people and asked them to repent. He warned them that the kingdom of God was coming. He pleaded for the people to get right with God. Some people chose to be baptized to show that they accepted John's message. His was a message of repentance.

One day John made King Herod angry. The king put John in jail. Rumors of a dead boy being raised back to life reached John's ears.

[Read Luke 18–28. Ask:]

- *Who came to Jesus with a question?* [two of John's disciples]
- *What was the question?* [Are You the Coming One, or should we look for another?]
- *While John's disciples were there, what did Jesus do?* [He healed the sick, those with evil spirits, and the blind.]
- *How did Jesus answer their question?* [He healed all of those people and then told the disciples to return to John and tell him all that they had seen.]
- *What did Jesus call John?* [a prophet; more than a prophet; the greatest prophet]
- *Why did He call John that?* [Jesus quoted Malachi 3:1 and claimed that John was the messenger who was to prepare the way before the Messiah.]

Let us review for a moment. In the Old Testament, God chose to speak to people directly, or to use specific people called prophets. There was nothing particularly special about this group of people. They could be men or women. They could be poor or rich, educated or not. What they all had in common was that God had chosen them to send a message to His people.

John had been given a special and specific message for anyone who would hear him, not just the Jews. The kingdom of God was coming! Be ready! Repent of your sin!

Repent means going one way and then deciding to turn around and go the other way.

[Illustrate this by standing and walking one way. Then stop, turn around, and walk back to where you were.]

Many prophets before John had delivered a similar message, but John's was different in one way.

John told the people to repent; they were to stop living their lives the way they were living them and turn to God's way of living instead. Why should they do that? Because the Messiah was coming. The Messiah was not coming sometime in the future anymore. No, the time was now.

He had an important message. John knew that Jesus was the Messiah. John had probably grown up with Jesus. They were cousins and six months apart in age. John had baptized Jesus and had witnessed the Spirit hovering on Him like a dove.

Sitting in a jail cell, John had started to doubt. We do not know how long he had been in jail, but it was long enough for him to send two friends to Jesus to find out if He really was the Messiah.

The man known as THE greatest prophet doubted Jesus was the Messiah. John needed reassurance that Jesus really was Who He claimed to be.

LIFE APPLICATION

[Read Isaiah 61:1–2. Ask:]

- *What does Isaiah tell us in these verses?* [The Spirit of the Lord is upon someone; the Lord anointed this person to preach to the poor, heal the brokenhearted, proclaim freedom to captives, and open prisons for those who are bound.]
- *Of whom do you think that verse is speaking?* [Jesus]

John would have known these verses in Isaiah. When Jesus answered John's disciples, He told them to tell John everything they had seen. Jesus had been preaching to the poor. He had been healing the sick, probably those with physical sickness and those with mental and emotional issues. He had freed people from the bonds of demons, and He had raised people from the prison of death.

Sometimes we can doubt like John. He was in jail, and he did not understand why the Messiah was not taking over and establishing the kingdom.

Sometimes things happen and we do not understand. Maybe a friend is mean to us. Maybe a parent or other loved one dies. Perhaps, because of a lack of finances, a family finds themselves living in a car. Maybe a house burns down, or a tornado destroys a school.

John did not understand what was going on. However, he knew Who to go to!

You can do that, too. When something happens and you do not understand why, go to Jesus and ask. You might get an answer like John did, telling you to remember Who Jesus is. He is the One who heals. He is the One.

Jesus said one other thing about John. He told the people that being a great prophet is not nearly as great as being a part of the kingdom of God. If you are a person who chooses to follow Jesus and be a part of His kingdom, then you have something all the Old Testament prophets, including John the Baptist, never had. They all died before Jesus died on the cross. You have the Law of God written on your spiritual heart.

Ezekiel talked about God giving people a new heart and a new spirit. This is what he was prophesying about! Jesus changes your heart and the Holy Spirit dwells with you.

The prophets never had that opportunity, but you do!

What is God saying through John the Baptist? Even the one described as the greatest prophet doubted Jesus. When you have doubts, Jesus can handle all of your questions.

COMMENT BOX

THINK: What went well as you taught this lesson? What can you do better?

_____
_____
_____
_____
_____
_____
_____
_____
_____
_____

TIP: Allow for a time of questioning. You could give each student paper to write on, or allow them to speak out loud. Choose one or two questions to discuss. LISTEN to the questions. They will help you know more about their hearts, and then you can teach them better.

30 JOHN THE REVELATOR

Many people see the book of Revelation as scary. While Revelation is filled with prophecy that is confusing, John still shared the same message that the prophets before him shared.

Scripture Focus: Revelation 4:6–11; Isaiah 6:2–3; Ezekiel 1:5–14; Daniel 7:3–7

Materials:

- White copy paper
- Crayons or colored pencils

Geography: Isle of Patmos; A.D. 95 or 96

Background: Most scholars believe that the book of Revelation was written by the Apostle John. There is some evidence that might prove otherwise, but most early church fathers refuted the evidence.

We must keep in mind that the book of Revelation (ONE revelation, not revelations) was a letter written to real churches. While there is prophecy that has not been fulfilled, we must study Revelation in historical and cultural contexts to help us understand this apocalyptic book. Even then, there is much we do not understand.

If we are to understand at least some of Revelation, then we must compare it to other apocalyptic books of Scripture, especially Daniel, Ezekiel, and Isaiah. This is one reason why learning about the prophets of the Old Testament is important. Reading the prophets helps Bible believers to have a cohesive understanding of the entire Bible narrative.

John has told everything that he has seen. It is the truth that Jesus Christ told him; it is the message from God.

— Revelation 1:2 (ICB)

OBJECT LESSON

[Put children in groups of three. Give each child one sheet of paper. Put a few crayons or colored pencils in the middle of each group of three. Instruct the children to carefully fold their paper into thirds (portrait, not landscape), unfold the paper, and place it vertically in front of them. Have them write their names on the very bottom of the paper. Say:]

When I say, *"Go,"* everyone will draw the head of an animal in the top third of your paper. Make sure the head fills the space. Do not make it tiny.

[Give the children thirty seconds to draw. Tell them to put their crayons down. Direct them to carefully fold back the third of the paper on which they drew so their drawing cannot be seen. Have the children hand their paper to the person on their right. Say:]

In this middle space, draw the body of a different animal. Do not draw the legs; only draw the body.

[Give them thirty seconds to draw. Tell them to put their crayons down. Direct them to carefully fold back the second third of the paper on which they drew so their drawing cannot be seen. Have the children hand their paper to the person on their right. Say:]

In this last space, draw the bottom portion of a different animal—maybe the feet, legs, and tail. Be sure to fill the space.

[Give them thirty seconds to draw. Tell them to put their crayons down and give the paper back to the owner. Have them unfold the paper to see a strange creature. Challenge them to name the new animal.]

You all created some crazy new animals! In fact, if we were to meet one of your animals in real life, it might be scary.

[Choose one of the animals drawn by the children. Have them imagine what it would be like to see the strange beast as real and standing in front of them. What sounds would they hear? How would the beast move? Would it talk? Would it be kind? Mean? Scared of people? Etc.]

BIBLE LESSON

Some of the prophets we have learned about had dreams and visions that included animals that might have been similar to the ones you drew.

[Read Isaiah 6:2–3. Ask:]

- *We have read these verses before in a previous lesson. Do you recall what happened next to Isaiah?* [Allow for answers. Use this as a moment to learn what your children remember about Isaiah's calling.]
- *What were the creatures that Isaiah saw in his vision?* [Seraphim]
- *How are they described?* [Each had six wings; two wings covered the faces, two covered the feet, and two were used for flying.]
- *What word do you see them saying three times?* [holy]

We know that if a word is used three times, then it must be important. These beasts were flying above God's throne and calling out, *"Holy! Holy! Holy!"*

Let us see if we can learn more about these creatures.

[Read Ezekiel 1:5–14. Ask:]

- *What do we learn about these four creatures?* [Allow the children to list off everything from the Scripture. If you have a white board or chalkboard, consider trying to draw the four creatures. Do not worry about being an artist. Draw the main descriptions for each one.]
- *How many wings did these creatures have?* [They had four wings. Two wings touched the others creatures, and two covered their bodies.]
- *What were these creatures doing?* [They went wherever the Holy Spirit told them to go.]
- *How did they move?* [Allow for answers. Perhaps they flew, but they could also run like lightning.]

These verses give us more information about these creatures. In the Isaiah verses, the creatures were in the throne room of God. In these verses, the creatures come out of a whirlwind. So far, these creatures are not doing anything scary, even though they may look scary and intimidating.

Let us see if another prophet saw these creatures.

[Read Daniel 7:3–7. Ask:]

- *Where do the creatures come from this time?* [They came up from the sea.]
- *What do these creatures look like?* [Allow for answers. Again, try to draw how these creatures may have looked.]

These four beasts looked similar in some ways and different in others. We also read about things happening to these beasts. Again, they sound like they looked strange and scary, but they are not doing anything to harm people or the prophet who witnessed the vision.

Let us see if there is anything else we can learn about these creatures.

[Read Revelation 4:6–10. Ask:]

- *Where are the creatures?* [in the throne room of God]
- *How are these described?* [Allow for answers. Have the children add details to any of the creatures you may have drawn already.]
- *What are these creatures doing?* [They do not rest; day and night they say "Holy, Holy, Holy," giving glory and honor and thanks to God.]
- *What happens when these creatures say these words?* [Twenty-four elders fall down before God on the throne and worship Him.]

Again, we have read that these scary-looking beasts do not harm anyone. In fact, they are showing us what to do.

LIFE APPLICATION

■ ■ ■ ■ ■ ■ ■ ■ ■ ■ ■ ■ ■ ■ ■ ■ ■ ■ ■

[Ask:]

- *God is holy. We have had quite a few prophets tell us that God is holy, but what does that really mean?* [Allow for answers.]

God is not like us humans. He is a different substance. He is more than we can imagine. We cannot begin to think about how powerful God is, or how kind He is, or how loving He is. Our minds are not made to truly understand the holiness of God.

Because of this, the Bible teaches us something called having the "fear of the Lord." Many of the prophets tried to get the Israelites to have a fear of the Lord.

The fear of the Lord does not mean to be scared of God. We cannot be scared of Someone who wants to have a special relationship with us. Remember, God wants to dwell with you all the time!

[Point to the creatures you drew.]

Think of those beasts and creatures. While they might seem scary, Scripture shows us that they worship God.

That was what God wanted from His chosen people, the Israelites. This is why God sent all of those prophets to them. He wanted to dwell with the people and have them worship Him.

This is what God wants from us. Choosing to believe in Jesus allows a holy God to dwell within you. And He will do whatever it takes to free you from any sin that is causing you to not worship Him with a full heart.

[Read 2 Peter 3:9. Ask:]

- *What does God not want to happen to us?* [He does not want us to perish.]
- *What does He want us to do?* [repent]

John the Revelator

- *How long will God wait?* [He will wait a long time; He is patient.]
- *Who else said a message similar to this?* [all of the prophets]

Most scholars think the book of Revelation was written by John the Apostle who walked with Jesus. He had the amazing blessing of seeing what would happen in the future. However, like many visions, John's visions do not make much sense.

This is why we went back to some of the other prophets to see if they had similar experiences as John.

All of the prophets have a message for you: God loves you. He wants to be with you and dwell with you forever. Before He can do that, you must repent and turn away from thinking, doing, and saying things that do not please Him.

Jesus is the only One who can help you do that. When you choose to allow Jesus to be your Master and Teacher, then God, the Holy Spirit, enters the heart of your spirit and dwells with you.

That is good news worth sharing!

Holy! Holy! Holy! God is worthy of our worship!

What is God saying through John? God is worthy of our worship because He is holy and patient with us. Like the beasts that the prophets described, we should, day and night, proclaim glory, honor, and thanks to God.

COMMENT BOX

THINK: What went well as you taught this lesson? What can you do better?

_____
_____
_____
_____
_____
_____
_____
_____
_____

TIP: Choose a worship hymn or song that focuses on the holiness of God, and teach it to your children.

31 NOW WE TAKE OVER

As our study of the prophets comes to a close, use this lesson to review messages from the prophets and to teach how we in the Church now carry the message of God to the world.

Scripture Focus: 1 Peter 1:10–12, 2:9

Materials:

- Megaphone (If you do not have one, you can make one out of cardstock by creating a cone and taping the paper together.)
- Airhorn (optional)

Geography: Jerusalem after Jesus resurrected and ascended to heaven

Background: Christian means "little Christ." If we say we are Christians, then we are to be and act like Christ. The prophets did not know when the Christ, the Messiah, was to come. It was through their faith that they obtained the hope of heaven. Hebrews 11 goes through many Old Testament saints, explaining how their faith in what was to come brought about their heavenly reward.

The prophets searched carefully and tried to learn about this salvation. They spoke about the grace that was coming to you.
—1 Peter 1:10 (ICB)

OBJECT LESSON

[If you use the airhorn, hit the button and make the loud noise. Hold up the megaphone and tell everyone you have an announcement to make. Be creative. Be funny. Get their attention.]

I have an announcement to make! Jesus gave me these words and I want to tell them to you! I cannot wait to tell you these words! They are so exciting and life-giving! I need everyone's attention!

[Proceed to describe how excited you are and how wonderful the words are. Then put down the megaphone. Say:]

I cannot tell you His words yet. Let's see if you can figure them out before I tell you what they are.

BIBLE LESSON

We have been learning about different prophets through the Old Testament.

[Ask:]

- *How many prophets can you name?* [Moses, Samuel, Nathan, Gad, Ahijah, Shemaiah, Jahaziel, Elijah, Elisha, Obadiah, Joel, Jonah, Amos, Hosea, Isaiah, Micah, Nahum, Zephaniah, Jeremiah, Habakkuk, Daniel, Ezekiel, Zechariah, Haggai, Malachi, John the Baptist, John the Apostle]
- *Can you remember some of the things the prophets said?* [Allow for answers. Use this time as a review to see how well the children remember; use clues from previous lessons if needed.]

We have discussed many topics that the prophets spoke about. We talked about God calling Israel to repent of their sin. We heard about God giving warnings to other nations because of their sin. We learned of experiences that the prophets had which showed the power of God. These are all great things. However, the main message many of the prophets described was the coming of the Messiah.

The prophets did not know when the Messiah would come. In fact, they studied their own writings and the writings of other prophets trying to figure out the mystery of the Messiah.

[Read 1 Peter 1:10–12. Ask:]

- *Of what did the prophets seek, ask, inquire, and search?* [salvation]
- *What did the prophets prophesy?* [the grace that would come to us as believers in Jesus]
- *What did the prophets want to know?* [when the appointed time for the Messiah would take place]
- *Who was indicating, or pointing them, to the coming of the Messiah?* [the Holy Spirit]

- *What did the prophets predict about Jesus?* [His sufferings and coming glory]
- *To whom were the prophets truly writing?* [to those who would live later and hear the gospel]
- *What do the angels want to do?* [They want to look into, or understand, salvation through Jesus; that is something angels will not take part in because they do not need to be saved from sin.]

All throughout the Old Testament the prophets received words from God to give to the people in their community or time period. At the same time, the prophets were exploring the mystery of the coming King, the Christ, the Messiah and telling the people of the One who would be coming.

Let's explore some Scriptures.

[If you have readers, assign the following Scriptures for them to read aloud. If not, read Exodus 19:5-7; Isaiah 43:20b-21; Luke 24:44-47; 1 Peter 2:9. Ask:]

- *(Exodus) What do we learn about Israel?* [If they obeyed God and kept His covenant, then they would be God's special people; Israel would be a kingdom of priests and a holy nation.]
- *(Isaiah) What do we learn about Israel?* [They are God's people, His chosen; they are a people God formed for Himself; they will declare His praise.]
- *(Luke) Jesus is speaking. What had to be fulfilled?* [all the things written in the Law of Moses and the Prophets and the Psalms that concerned Jesus, the Messiah]
- *Because those things had to be fulfilled, what had to happen?* [Christ had to suffer and rise on the third day; repentance needed to be preached to all nations.]
- *(Peter) Peter is talking to the Church. What does he call it?* [a chosen generation; royal priesthood; holy nation; God's special people]
- *What are these people to do?* [proclaim the praises of Jesus]
- *Why?* [because Jesus saved us from the darkness of sin and brought us into the marvelous light of righteousness]

Now We Take Over

[Pick up the megaphone and say:]

WOW!

That is good news!!! The wonderful words everyone needs to hear are: Jesus loves them and died to save them from their sins. When we choose to believe that and follow Jesus, then we need to proclaim the praises of God and what He did for us to everyone.

LIFE APPLICATION

Way back in the book of Exodus, God saved the Hebrew people from the slavery of Egypt. Moses received the Law which set up Israel as God's special nation. It was to be a new, holy nation that showed God's characteristics and qualities to the nations around it. The Ten Commandments set Israel apart from other nations.

Israel still is God's chosen nation. However, God wanted all nations to come back to Him.

God sent Jesus. Jesus saves us from the slavery of sin. The greatest commandment is to love God with all our heart, soul, mind, and strength. The second commandment is to love our neighbors as we love ourselves. When we obey those two commands of Jesus, then we are holy and set apart from other people. We are a part of a new nation of people, a new priesthood. We are new creations through Christ.

That is good news! We need to tell people about Jesus.

We do not have to use a megaphone to do it, though.

[Ask:]

- *What are some ways we can follow the two commands Jesus gives us?* [Allow for answers. Lead them to think of ways to love God, obey parents, love people, and serve others, no matter who they are.]

Your faith in what Jesus did for you is what saves you from your sins. That should motivate you to proclaim His praises to people around you. Sometimes you can use words. Other times you can serve others.

In everything we think, say, or do, we should do it all for the glory of God.

What is God saying through the prophets? The prophets eagerly awaited the Messiah. He has come. Jesus died and rose again. And now WE get to proclaim the message of Jesus to the world.

COMMENT BOX

THINK: What went well as you taught this lesson? What can you do better?

_____
_____
_____
_____
_____
_____
_____
_____
_____

TIP: Share this quote with your students and discuss what it means and how it relates to sharing Jesus with others. *"There is a group of people who will only respond to your voice when it comes to your message; and if you don't put your message out there, they may never get the message."* ~ Ray Edwards

EXTRA RESOURCES

HOW TO LEAD A CHILD TO CHRIST

As you teach a Bible lesson, there are times when the Spirit leads you to ask the children if they want to follow Jesus through faith. Consider having those who want to make some sort of decision leave the larger groups of kids. Do this because it causes the child to physically make a decision: *"Do I stay? Or not?"* This also allows for fewer distractions. (Always be sure to have another adult nearby. That's a safety rule!) You could have the children stay behind while the others leave, or take the small group into another room.

Ask many questions; you want the children to think through what they are doing. These questions should not be answered by *"Yes," "No,"* or *"Jesus."* Use lots of Scripture, because you want God's Word to be working.

There is no minimum age for salvation. Even three-year-olds can recognize they are sinners and be sorry for what they do. However, you do want to be sure that the child, no matter the age, understands this lifelong commitment to Jesus.

Salvation is a big deal, and you do not want a child to make a decision that is not understood or taken seriously. If at any point you sense that there is confusion or uncertainty on the child's part, say, *"I can see that God is working in your heart. I want you to keep listening and learning. Let's tell your parents you want to learn more."* Then either take that child to his or her parents right away or after class.

Examples of Counseling Questions and Scripture to Read:

- Why have you decided to talk with me?
- Why do you need Jesus as your Savior?
- What is sin?
- What are some examples of sin?
- Can you do anything to get rid of sin?
- Read Romans 3:23.
- Who is Jesus?
- What did Jesus do for you?
- Read 1 Corinthians 15:3–4.
- Read John 3:16 or Acts 16:31.
- Would you like to pray to God and tell Him about your faith in Jesus?

If the child understands the questions, is serious about dealing with sin, and wanting to live for Jesus, explain that he or she needs to talk to God and that talking to God is called prayer.

At this point, if possible, go get the child's parents, or guardians. This is a special and personal time they can have with their child. Have the parents lead the child in prayer. However, sometimes a parent, or child, will not know what to pray. There is not one specific prayer that needs to be said. There are no magic words, but you can lead them to think through these questions and tell God the answers (possible answers are listed):

- What do you believe about yourself? [a sinner; unrighteous; need forgiveness]
- What do you believe about Jesus? [Jesus is God's Son. He died on the cross, rose again, and will come back. Jesus makes me right before God. Jesus took my sin.]
- What do you want Jesus to do for you? [make right with God; forgive sins; save from sin]

Once the child has prayed, read Hebrews 13:5b and 6a. Ask, *"What has Jesus done for you?"* This will give assurance of salvation.

Rejoice with the family!

It is possible you might have a situation that includes parents who are not happy about the choice made by their child. If this happens, explain the decision to the parents, but then, if at all possible, disciple that child yourself. If the child goes to another church or no church at all, check on the child when you can. Definitely pray for that young Christian.

Be sure to tell your pastor of the child's decision so he can follow up with the family and discuss baptism.

If you are a parent and your child has accepted Jesus as his or her Savior, be sure to help your child grow in knowledge and service.

** Consider giving the child a copy of *Mateo's Choice* to help disciple him and share the gospel with his family.

HOW TO BECOME AN EXCELLENT BIBLE TEACHER

When teaching children, our goal is two-fold. First, we want kids to **get right** with God through a saving faith. Second, we want our children to **stay right** with God through the sanctification process.

> You, however, continue in the things you have learned and become convinced of, knowing from whom you have learned them, and that from childhood you have known the sacred writings which are able to give you the wisdom that leads to salvation through faith which is in Christ Jesus. All Scripture is inspired by God and profitable for teaching, for reproof, for correction, for training in righteousness; so that the man of God may be adequate, equipped for every good work.
>
> 2 Timothy 3:14-17 (NASB)

WHAT We Want to Teach:

We want to focus on verse 16, because if we can (1) **teach** doctrine in a way that reveals sin, and then (2) explain how to turn from sin (**reproof**), and then (3) counsel children to go to Jesus to fix their sin problem (**correction**), THEN (4) through faith in Jesus, they will be restored to a character of **righteousness** so God can use them for good works. All of this happens through the power of the Holy Spirit.

Once we choose to follow Jesus, the Holy Spirit guides us through the process, or cycle, of sanctification using scripture. He teaches us more, reveals sin, shows us how to correct that sin, and leads us to become perfect as Jesus is perfect. However, the cycle of sanctification does not revolve in a circle. It is more like a spiral. As we grow closer to God and He works on our hearts, then we become closer to the center, or place of total perfection. We will not ever reach perfection this side of heaven, but we are on a journey with God to walk on His path of righteousness.

We can also think of it this way: As our view of God increases, our view of ourselves decreases. (Sounds like John the Baptist!) He must increase. We must decrease. Yes, we are children of God and heirs to a Kingdom, but we recognize we **were** unrighteous people and now **are** clothed in the righteousness of Jesus. We do not think less of ourselves (we are children of God!) but we become humbler in spirit and the discrepancy between us and Jesus is seen more and more. Jesus becomes bigger in our lives the more we know of Him and we recognize we need Him every minute of every day.

This is what we want for our children, whether they are our own or those we teach in the church. **We want them to view Jesus as being the One and Only Greatest Person in their lives.**

HOW We Teach This:

In order to be an excellent Bible teacher, a person must seek God first and foremost. **I fail at this.** I am not an excellent Bible teacher because of what I do, but because of what God chooses to do through me. I attempt to read the Bible every day. I attempt to make good choices. I mess up. I sin.

I think this is what makes the difference between a mediocre Bible teacher and an excellent Bible teacher: **An excellent Bible teacher daily recognizes his or her own need for a Savior**.

It is through our failings that Christ shines His light into our Bible lessons. When we explain to children how God is real, forgiving, and personal in our own lives, they will begin to search for that type of relationship as well.

How do we teach children? By allowing God to teach us. This means we need to take an honest look at ourselves, evaluate our hearts, and apply what God shows us to our teaching.

**For a more detailed approach to assessing and evaluating your ministry and teaching consider using the book *Distinctively Christian: A Christ-centered Worldview Approach to Elementary Ministry* by Milton V. Uecker, Ed. D. and Anne Marie Gosnell, M. Ed.

Prayerfully read through the next few questions and answer them.

Evaluation of Yourself:

1. Do you live in a manner worthy of your calling?
2. Do you exemplify humility, empathy, hospitality, compassion, and kindness?
3. Are you interested in your children's lives?
4. Can you sense the needs of your children?
5. Are you a servant leader?

Evaluation of Each Bible Lesson:

1. Did you accomplish your objectives?
2. If not, why?
3. What was weak?
4. What was strong?
5. What changes should you make before the next lesson or before you teach this lesson again?

Evaluation of the Teaching Year:

1. Does your church have purpose, mission, and vision statements?
2. Did your lessons reflect those statements?
3. Can you see a growth of Biblical knowledge and concepts in your children?
4. Do you see evidence of Christ-centered values and attitudes?
5. How have you trained parents or involved them in your teaching process?

> "To whom would He teach knowledge,
> And to whom would He interpret the message?
> Those just weaned from milk?
> Those just taken from the breast?
> "For He says, 'Order on order, order on order,
> Line on line, line on line, A little here, a little there.'"
>
> Isaiah 28:9-10 (NASB)

Biblical knowledge, or learning the Scriptures, takes a lifetime. It involves a little truth here and a little lesson there, step by step. We Bible teachers want our children to be convinced in their minds to follow God, so that they will be committed to God regardless of any obstacles. All of this happens through the power of the Holy Spirit. **A committed will to obey God equals a changed life.**

Keep the object lessons going! You can find all of the other books in the Object Lessons for Kids series on Amazon or futureflyingsaucers.com.

A NOTE FROM THE AUTHOR

■ ■ ■ ■ ■ ■ ■ ■ ■ ■ ■ ■ ■ ■ ■ ■ ■ ■ ■ ■

Friend, I encourage you. You hold the living, powerful Word of God in your hands. Use it wisely. Read it lovingly. Teach from it enthusiastically. Love powerfully. **Be Excellent!!**

Your Servant,

Anne Marie
FutureFlyingSaucers.com

PS. Did you like this book? Please leave a review on the platform of your choice or email me at futureflyingsaucers@klopex.com and tell me your thoughts. How did the children respond? Did you enjoy teaching these lessons? I want to know.

COLORING PAGES

In the past God spoke
to our ancestors
through the prophets.
He spoke to them many times
and in many different ways.
—Hebrews 1:1 (ICB)

FUTUREFLYINGSAUCERS.COM

The Lord was with Samuel
as he grew up. He did not let
any of Samuel's messages
fail to come true.

—1 Samuel 3:19 (ICB)

Then Nathan said to David,
"You are the man!"
—2 Samuel 12:7 (ICB)

The Lord told Gad,
"Go and tell David,
'This is what the Lord says:
I offer you three choices.
Choose one for me to do to you.'"

—2 Samuel 24:12 (ICB)

One day Jeroboam
was leaving Jerusalem.
Ahijah, the prophet from Shiloh,
met him on the road.
Ahijah was wearing a new coat.
The two men were alone
out in the country.
—1 Kings 11:29 (ICB)

Then Shemaiah the prophet
came to Rehoboam and
the leaders of Judah.
They had gathered in Jerusalem
because they were afraid of Shishak.
—2 Chronicles 12:5 (ICB)

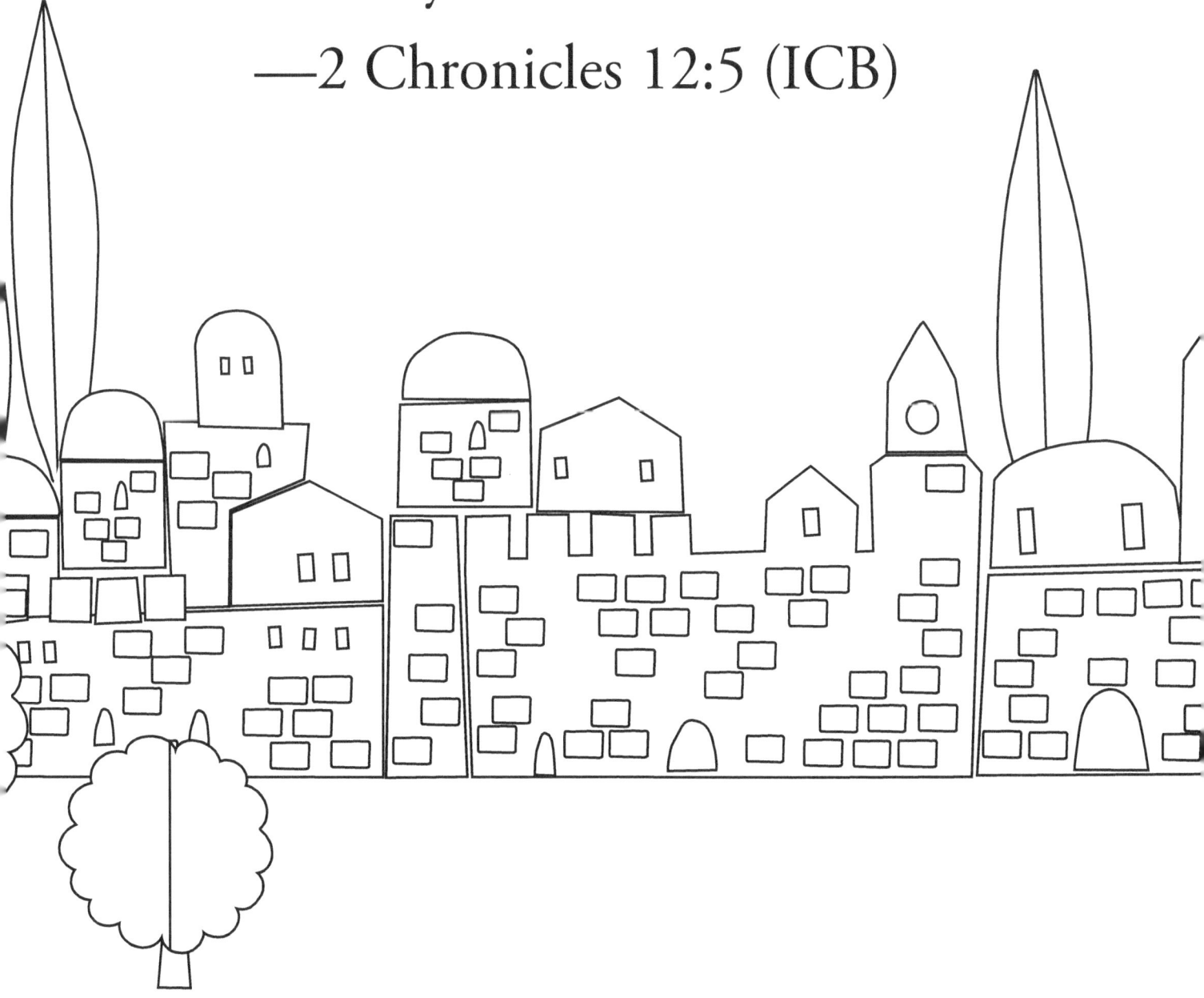

"Lord, answer my prayer.
Show these people that you, Lord, are God.
Then the people will know that you are
bringing them back to you."

—1 Kings 18:37 (ICB)

Elijah and Elisha were still walking and talking.
Then a chariot and horses of fire appeared.
The chariot and horses of fire separated Elijah from Elisha.
Then Elijah went up to heaven in a whirlwind.

—2 Kings 2:11 (ICB)

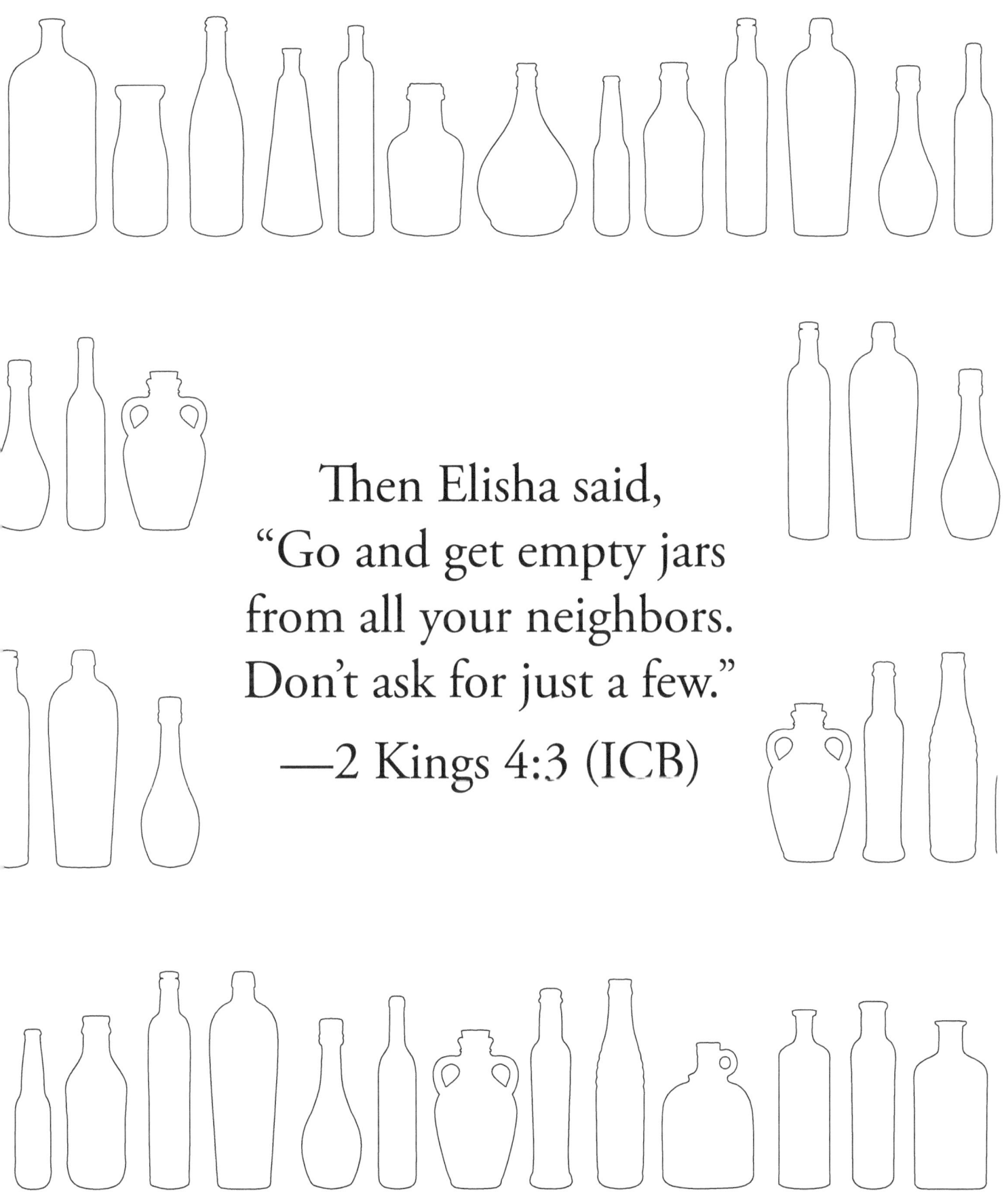

Then Elisha said, "Go and get empty jars from all your neighbors. Don't ask for just a few."
—2 Kings 4:3 (ICB)

One day Elisha went to Shunem.
An important woman lived there.
She begged Elisha to stay and eat.
So every time Elisha passed by,
he stopped there to eat.

—2 Kings 4:8 (ICB)

The Lord's day of judging
is coming soon to all the nations.
You did evil things to other people.
Those same things will happen to you.
They will come back upon your own head.

— Obadiah 1:15 (ICB)

"After this, I will give my Spirit
freely to all kinds of people.
Your sons and daughters
will prophesy . . .
At that time I will give
my Spirit even to servants,
both men and women.

— Joel 2:28-29 (ICB)

So the men cried to the Lord, "Lord, please don't let us die because of taking this man's life…Lord, you have caused all this to happen. You wanted it this way."

—Jonah 1:14 (ICB)

The Lord said to him,
"Go, and marry a woman
who will be unfaithful to you.
She will give you children
whose fathers are other men.

— Hosea 1:2 (ICB)

A child will be born to us. God will give a son to us. He will be responsible for leading the people. His name will be Wonderful Counselor, Powerful God, Father Who Lives Forever, Prince of Peace.

— Isaiah 9:6 (ICB)

But you, Bethlehem Ephrathah,
are one of the smallest towns in Judah.
But from you will come one who will
rule Israel for me. He comes from
very old times, from days long ago.

— Micah 5:2 (ICB)

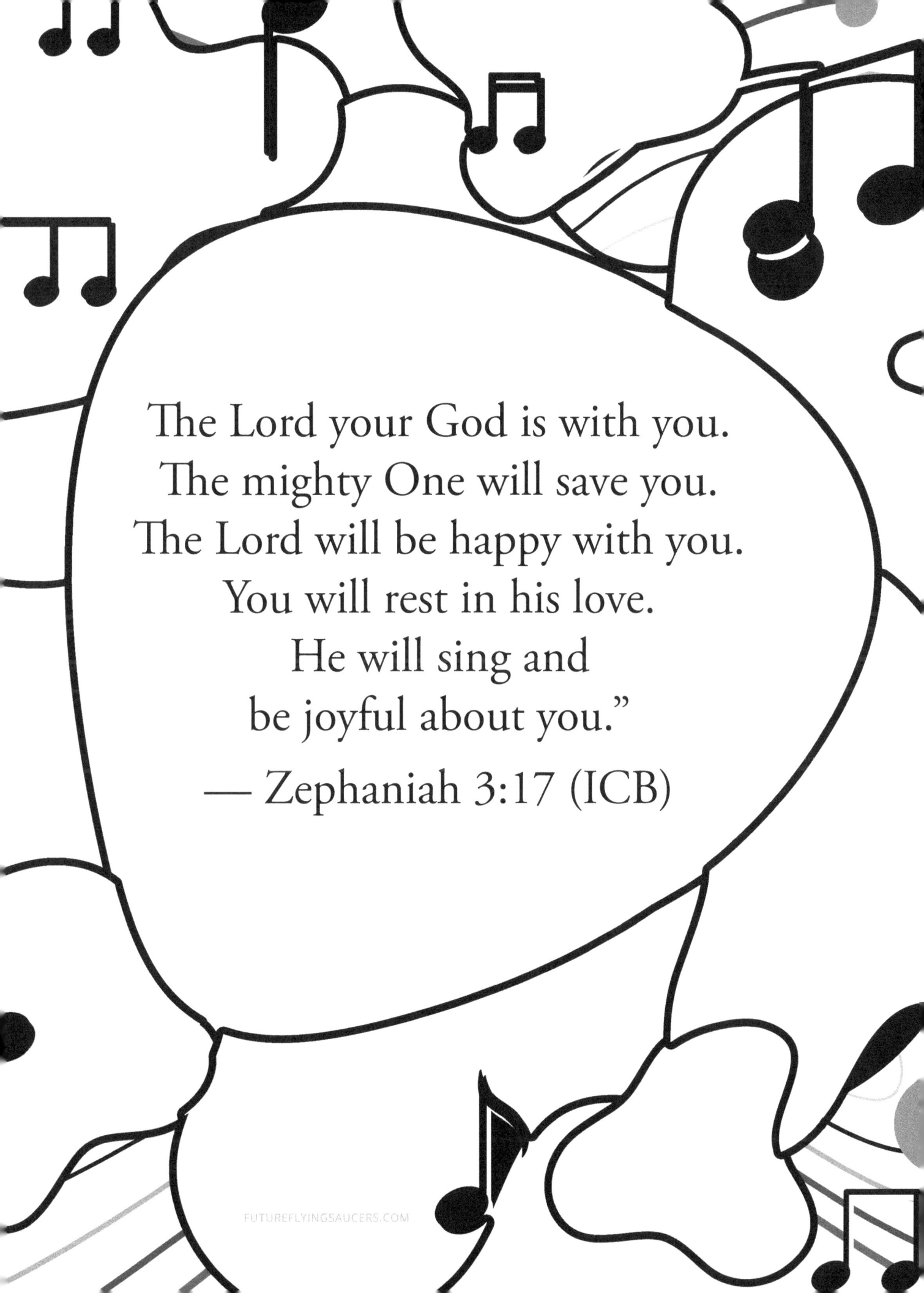

Jeremiah, get a scroll.
Write on it all the words I have spoken to you about Israel and Judah and all the nations. Write everything I have spoken to you since Josiah was king until now.

— Jeremiah 36:2 (ICB)

Your eyes are too good to look at evil. You cannot stand to see people do wrong. So how can you put up with those evil people? How can you be quiet when wicked people defeat people who are better than they are?

— Habakkuk 1:13 (ICB)

MENE, MENE, TEKEL, UPHARSIN

"I have heard that you are
able to explain what things mean.
And you can find the answers
to hard problems.
Read this writing on the wall
and explain it to me."

— Daniel 5:16 (ICB)

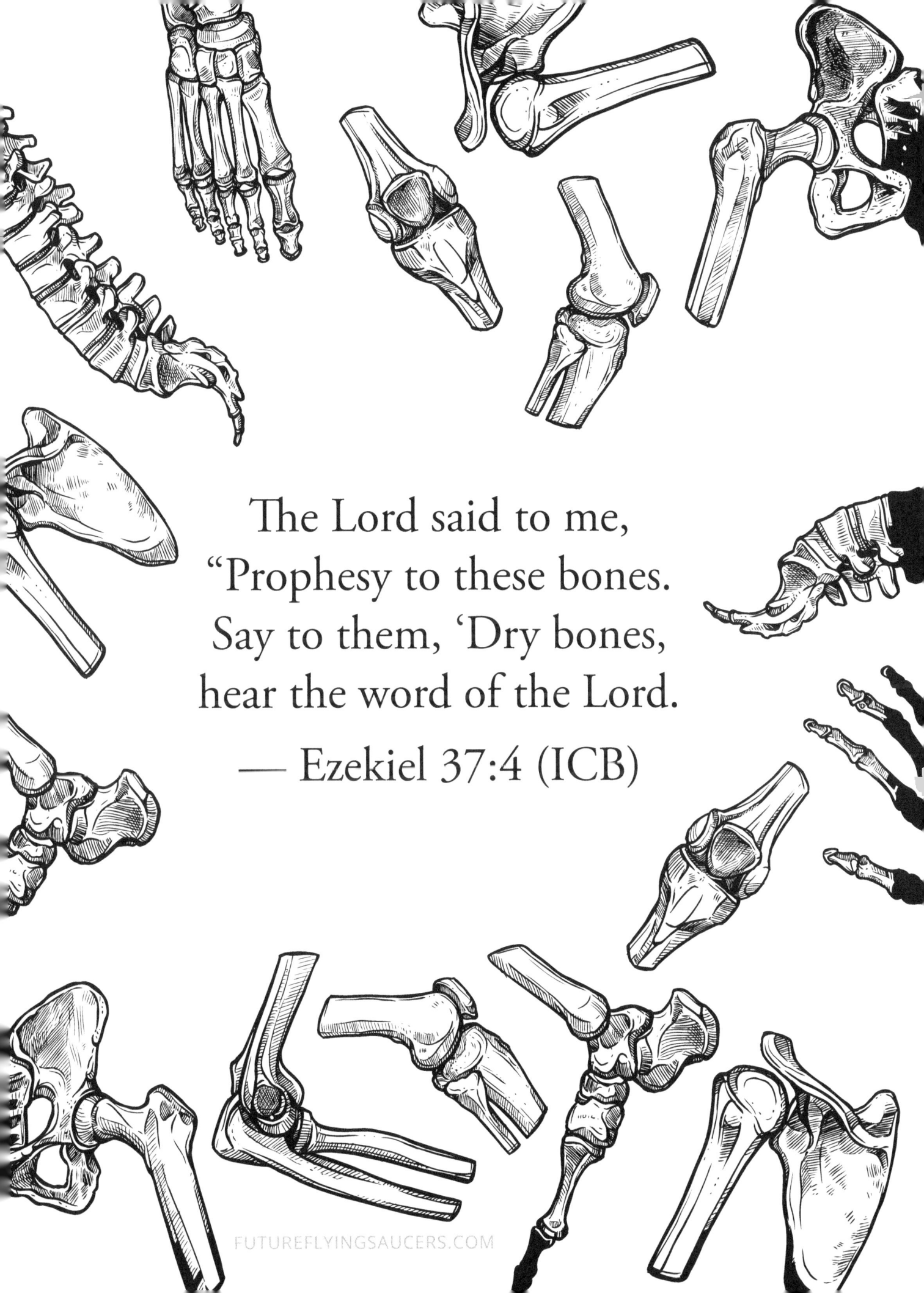

I made a promise to you
when you came out of Egypt.
My Spirit is still with you.
So don't be afraid.

— Haggai 2:5 (ICB)

"Shout and be glad, Jerusalem. I am coming, and I will live among you," says the Lord.

— Zechariah 2:10 (ICB)

The Lord of heaven's armies says,
"I will send my messenger.
He will prepare the way for me to come.
Suddenly, the Lord you are looking for
will come to his Temple.
The messenger of the agreement,
whom you want, will come."

— Malachi 3:1 (ICB)

But what did you go out to see? A prophet?
Yes, and I tell you, John is more than a prophet.
This was written about John:
'I will send my messenger ahead of you.
He will prepare the way for you.'

— Luke 7:26-27 (ICB)

futureflyingsaucers.com

John has told everything that he has seen. It is the truth that Jesus Christ told him; it is the message from God.

— Revelation 1:2 (ICB)

The prophets searched carefully
and tried to learn about this salvation.
They spoke about the grace that was coming to you.

—1 Peter 1:10 (ICB)